MOMS WHO HIKE

MOMS WHO HIKE

Walking with America's Most Inspiring Adventurers

HEATHER BALOGH ROCHFORT

FALCON®

Guilford, Connecticut

An imprint of The Rowman & Littlefield Publishing Group, Inc.
4501 Forbes Blvd., Ste. 200
Lanham, MD 20706
www.rowman.com

Falcon and FalconGuides are registered trademarks and Make Adventure Your Story is a trademark of The Rowman & Littlefield Publishing Group, Inc.
Distributed by NATIONAL BOOK NETWORK

British Library Cataloguing-in-Publication Information available

Library of Congress Cataloging-in-Publication Data

Names: Rochfort, Heather Balogh, author.
Title: Moms who hike : walking with America's most inspiring adventurers / Heather Balogh Rochfort.
Description: Guilford, Connecticut : Falcon Guides, 2021.
Identifiers: LCCN 2020052932 (print) | LCCN 2020052933 (ebook) | ISBN 9781493058280 (paperback) | ISBN 9781493058297 (epub)
Subjects: LCSH: Women hikers—United States—Biography. | Mothers—United States—Biography. | Hiking—United States. | Hiking—Psychological aspects.
Classification: LCC GV191.5 .R64 2021 (print) | LCC GV191.5 (ebook) | DDC 796.51085/2—dc23
LC record available at https://lccn.loc.gov/2020052932
LC ebook record available at https://lccn.loc.gov/2020052933

∞™ The paper used in this publication meets the minimum requirements of American National Standard for Information Sciences—Permanence of Paper for Printed Library Materials, ANSI/NISO Z39.48-1992.

The author and The Rowman & Littlefield Publishing Group, Inc. assume no liability for accidents happening to, or injuries sustained by, readers who engage in the activities described in this book.

Contents

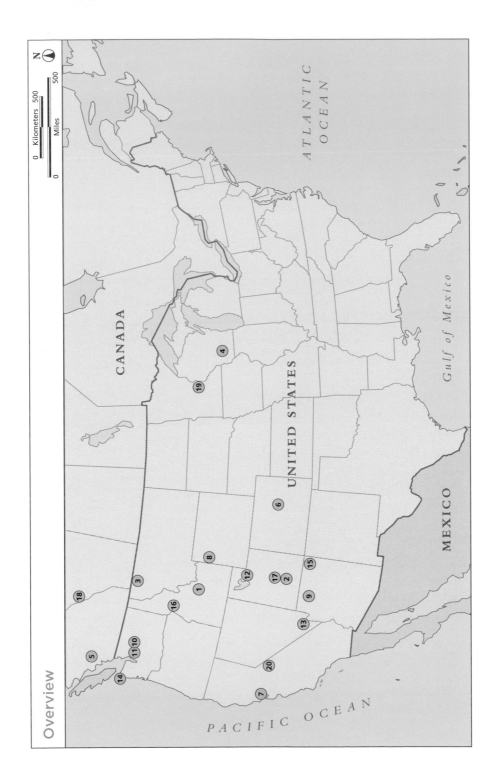

Overview

Foreword

We already know hiking is good for kids. Peer-reviewed research shows a strong positive association between children spending time in nature and overall health and cognitive development. And we already know hiking is good for women. Decreasing stress, strengthening muscles, and increasing cardiovascular fitness are just a few benefits women experience when they spend time on the trail.

But the *why* behind *moms* who choose to hike is often much, much deeper than any data-backed research or health statistic.

Motherhood can be a beautifully exhausting, all-consuming, and often lonely journey. We give and we give, and then we give and give some more. Somewhere between wiping jelly off the arm of the couch, rushing somebody to the bus stop, and muting our end of a work Zoom call because one of the kids is crying for mama, we find ourselves needing to be nurtured. That's right: Moms need to be nurtured too.

Maybe that's why so many of us moms hike. Maybe that's why you picked this book up for yourself. Maybe you need to be nurtured.

Heather and I met on a ladies' hut trip in Colorado's San Juan Mountains in 2016. I was a single mom and planned a road trip with a girlfriend to meet up with some like-minded women for an adventure in the mountains. At the time, I was the only mother on the trip, but the mountains were our equalizer. We all hiked and played board games and stayed up late bonding around the campfire. Somewhere between our hike to a stunningly blue lake and stretching downward dog in the hut, I found restoration and rejuvenation that I hadn't experienced in months. It's hard to prioritize self-care when you are stressing about your little one eating enough vegetables, getting enough sleep, and that last bout of diaper rash. But I found it in those days of high-alpine exploration.

I was instantly attracted to Heather because of the quiet and steady way she hung back and supported others. Sure, she was knowledgeable about the mountains we were moving through. But I noticed that she stayed back with the women who needed support and friendship. Even before becoming a mother, she approached adventure with a nurturing and patient spirit.

It was my first time leaving my son to travel out of state, and I rushed home early when I learned he had an ear infection. But long after I returned home, the late nights around the fire with the group of open-hearted women stayed in the forefront of my mind. Meaningful experiences outside give us fortitude as we approach the unique challenges of motherhood. Those nights around the fire in the San Juans planted the seeds for a long-lasting friendship.

Fast forward a few years and I was pregnant with my second child and moving to Denver, Colorado. Heather was now a mother to a very outgoing and curious one-year-old daughter. The two of us stayed in touch on social media and I was grateful to have a friend in our new home state to meet for playdates on the trail. I curiously watched to see how Heather adapted to her outdoors lifestyle with a baby in tow. Spoiler alert: She brought her adventurous spirit to motherhood and absolutely flourished as a new mom. Heather and her husband, Will, changed diapers in the backcountry, skied into yurts with their infant, bike-packed as a family through mountains, and traveled to exotic lands all before their daughter's first birthday. They literally wrote the book about camping with kids and I've enjoyed watching from afar and up close.

Despite the extraordinary family adventures, the international travel, and juggling an impressive career, I might admire Heather most for hand pumping on a via ferrata in Italy. Any mother knows hand pumping is a labor of love—especially when it's done on the side of a sheer cliff. But what I appreciate even more than her example of motherhood in the outdoors is the way Heather opened up a vulnerable and honest dialogue around the challenges of breastfeeding and how our expectations about being a mother aren't always a reality. She continues to break down those barriers that often feel isolating to mothers. Maybe that's the magic that happens on the trail: Barriers dissolve when we feel vulnerable, and we connect in a more meaningful way.

You see, Heather seeks to uplift, celebrate, include, educate, and bring other mothers along with her. Just like that first hut trip when I met her years ago, Heather is the friend who quietly hangs back and supports the one who needs a friend.

That's what you can expect from *Moms Who Hike*. Whether you're an athlete like world-renowned hiker Jennifer Pharr Davis, learning to find a new pace on the trail after becoming a mom, or a mother looking to reclaim part of herself by finding a new love for hiking like Shon't Savage, you will find a relatable woman in these pages. Maybe you're a mom like me. In the book I share how my failure on the trail taught me to find beauty in this oh-so-short season of life.

You see, we weren't designed to do this whole motherhood thing alone. We look to each other for friendship, companionship, and encouragement. While turning the pages of *Moms Who Hike*, you'll find inspiration. But much more importantly, you'll find an invitation.

—Brooke Murray

Acknowledgments

I'm overflowing with gratitude for the twenty women featured within these pages, each of whom dedicated hours of their precious "free time" to speak with me on the phone and answer question after question after question. As a mother myself, I understand that spare time is limited and I'm profusely thankful that they were willing to give some of theirs to me and this project. It's not easy to balance work, family, life, and personal interests, but each of you do it with grace and class. I admire you all immensely.

I'm forever grateful to two women in particular: Erica and Sarah. Without these women's dedication and assistance, I dare say I'd still be curled up in a ball on the floor of my office, willing this book into existence rather than accomplishing anything.

As always, I owe everything to my husband, Will. He's been along for the ride on a number of my book projects and he handles each one with clarity and patience—two skills I'm severely lacking and wish I could acquire from him through osmosis. I know I'm not the easiest person to cohabitate with—especially on a looming deadline—so thank you for being my eternal rock in this life.

I'd be remiss if I didn't mention my own mother. Her undying tenacity and indomitable spirit routinely led us to the trails when I was a kid. While I certainly didn't appreciate those nature walks at the time, I cherish the memories as an adult.

Finally, of course, my undying love goes to our daughter, Liliana. At some point she may tire of seeing her name in the acknowledgments of my books, but I still won't stop including it. Without you, I would not be a mother and could never have conceived of this wild ride called parenthood. You are strong; you are kind; you are smart; and you are loved. And I thank you every day for choosing me to be your mama, baby girl.

Introduction

In 2017, my husband and I welcomed our daughter into this world. She came in with a ferocity and zest for life that has since proven to be her norm. With her arrival came a new chapter of my life, and I quickly learned that nothing could prepare me for motherhood. Thanks to a tumultuous childbirth and subsequent troubles in the first months, I went from a "hardcore outdoor woman" to a mentally and physically broken mother who wasn't sure which end was up. I loved our little bundle of joy more than my own life, but I still struggled to navigate my new reality.

Sleepless days blended into months as I gradually crawled my way back into the real world. But looking back on it, I don't think I fully rediscovered myself again until she was nearly seven months old. Thanks to a wonderful parental leave policy, my husband had 4 months of paid paternity leave that he was allowed to use within the first year of our daughter's life. After using 6 weeks after she was born, we saved the remaining allotment for a 3-month-long road trip through the American West. We left Denver in May and did not return until early August. In that time, we traveled everywhere and we traveled nowhere. We lived in a tent and cooked our meals on the tailgate of our F-150 pickup. We posted up in dispersed campsites outside of Capitol Reef National Park and near the North Rim of the Grand Canyon. We even found our way to her first multi-night backpacking trip, a 5-night epic journey to California's Thousand Island Lake where our dear friends packed out more than 10 pounds of dirty diapers in a dry bag. (Yes, we're still friends, and yes, we still owe them.) We learned how to wash bottles in the backcountry and how to deal with major diaper rash in canyon country.

More than anything, I learned how to move forward as a mother. This road trip was my catalyst, my springboard, which allowed me to clearly see how I could combine my old life with my new one. But I also know not everyone has such a bizarre opportunity in their lives (nor would most want to dirtbag it with an infant) to recalibrate and adjust. Being a mother is an incredibly special, life-affirming honor, and I continue to be amazed at how women navigate the privilege with grace.

No one gives you a manual when you become a mom, and if you want to make that transition in the outdoors, it's even tougher. (Do me a favor and Google "How to take your infant backpacking" and you'll see a mish-mash of half-baked information, including a majority advising against such "dangerous" activities.) Each woman highlighted in the pages of this book epitomizes a grander look at what it takes to be a mother in the outdoors. From first-generation Americans to celebrated long-distance powerhouses, professional athletes to online influencers, emergency psychiatrists to stay-at-home moms, CEOs of beer companies to social justice advocates, there is a mother in here that looks like you. And perhaps she is experiencing outdoor motherhood like you are right now.

Each mama shares a memorable anecdote from her time in the trenches. For some, the story is a poignant remembrance of how hiking saved her mental health, but for others, it's simply a fond memory cobbled together from the sweet day-to-day instances that comprise parenthood. Because we all know one thing for certain: Motherhood doesn't look the same on two people. And motherhood in the outdoors is only the beginning of a wild ride, one that I hope you will find inspiration for within the pages of this book.

Buckle up, my friends.

—Heather Balogh Rochfort

How to Use This Guide

This guidebook is by no means a comprehensive resource and it certainly cannot answer every single question you have about your planned hike. But then again, that is the beauty of hiking: the mystery you uncover around every bend in the trail.

Each mother highlighted in this book chose a special trail, which means you will find a wide variety of treks. Most hikes are as short as a few miles, easily accessible for families with small children or parents looking to carry a child in a kid carrier. This book is a choose-your-own adventure of hiking fun, but it is your responsibility to choose a trail best suited for your abilities and those of your family.

Included with each route description are helpful pieces of information such as approximate hiking time, length, elevation gain, trails used, and special considerations. Driving directions and GPS coordinates are provided for the trailheads to each hike as well. Finally, a basic map is provided with trails, distances, and key points along the route. Each hiker is different and I understand that hiking times will vary widely from person to person, so I tried to estimate ballpark time frames as best as possible. Then again, your toddler may be faster than my own.

TYPES OF TRIPS

There are three categories of hikes you will see in this book:

Out-and-Back: This means you will hike to a specific destination and then turn around to retrace your steps back to the trailhead.

Loop: This type of hike begins and ends at the same location with minimal retracing of your steps. If you look at the corresponding map, you will see that your route follows a loop-shaped pattern. In at least one instance, you will see the term "lollipop loop" used to describe a trail. This means you will hike for a distance, then complete a loop before retracing your steps back to the trailhead.

Point-to-Point: This type of hike is a one-way journey, meaning you begin at one trailhead and conclude at another. Frequently, this calls for a car shuttle or another means of transportation to return you from whence you came.

DIFFICULTY RATINGS

It is hard to standardize ratings of trail difficulty since they are largely subjective and depend on the individual, her fitness levels, and the required number of snack breaks. That said, I tried to standardize each hike as best as I could to help prepare you for your adventures. In doing so, I used three categorizations:

Easy trails are suitable for any hiker. This includes families with children, the elderly, and anyone who is hoping to learn more about hiking. Elevation gain is minimal and you will encounter very few trail hazards. Navigation is almost nonexistent and you will never have to go off-trail.

Moderate trails are suitable for any hiker who has some experience outdoors and on the trail. You will need an average fitness level to complete a moderate hike and specific sections may still challenge you. Occasional route-finding may be required and you can expect elevation gain to range from 1,000 to 2000 feet over the course of the trail.

Strenuous trails are the most challenging hikes you will find in this book. These are meant for very experienced outdoorists who have a high level of fitness and confidence in their abilities. The trail may be difficult to find at times and/or route-finding could be required. Off-trail hiking is also a possibility. Sections of a strenuous trail may be very exhausting and you can expect to find more than 2,000 feet of elevation gain on this category of trail.

TRAIL USE

Most trails in this book are suitable for three types of athletes: hikers, backpackers, or trail runners. In reality, the only difference between the three is that backpackers spend the night on the trail while the other two categories usually opt to return home. Backpackers prefer longer routes to justify camping outside whereas day hikers frequently opt for less distance. You will see all three categories of athlete on these trails, so be sure to smile and wave, even if your kid is experiencing a full-scale meltdown. After all, you are out there enjoying Mother Nature . . . and parents just get it, so no need to feel ashamed.

PERMITS AND FEES

Various land-management agencies utilize permits and fee structures, so you will see this vary from trail to trail. These fees and policies frequently change depending on the political climate and/or trail usage, so it is best to do research before leaving home. Call ahead to the local ranger station to be sure you don't show up to a trailhead empty-handed and permit-less when one is required.

And if you know permits are called for yet you don't have one? Be kind; do not bandit the trail. Sure, it is possible that you will not get caught, but permits are in place for a reason and it is not because rangers enjoy policing our nation's trails. Permits frequently regulate the quantity of visitors to help preserve our trails, so follow the rules. This makes the wilderness a safer place for everyone.

Before You Hit the Trail

WEATHER AND SEASONS

Weather is the great equalizer of hiking. It does not matter how fit you are or how much you enjoy the trail; poor weather can ruin a trip if you are unprepared. Plan ahead by doing your research from home. Watch the weather weeks in advance and as your trip draws closer, paying special attention to the weather patterns on your specific hike. Rainy weather is not always a reason to call off a trip, but communicate with others in your group. You may feel comfortable hiking through rain for three days but your partners may not. Additionally, consider your altitude and topographical location if you see nasty weather in the forecast. Rainstorms above the tree line frequently bring lightning and thunder, both meteorological occurrences that can be deadly. Some hikes are prone to lightning strikes, so double check the weekend forecast before hitting the dirt.

Trail seasonality is highly subjective. For example, Havasu Falls in Arizona is going to look much different than Colorado's Pikes Peak when January rolls around. Typically, summer is the best season for hiking in the West and at higher altitudes whereas southerners prefer winter or spring to escape the fiery hot and muggy conditions.

If you plan on hiking a high-altitude trail, keep the cooler temperatures in mind. In Colorado, for example, it could be 85 degrees and sunny at the trailhead but 55 degrees and sleeting a few thousand feet up. Additionally, snow lasts much longer as you climb higher in the mountains, so plan on encountering a few snowfields if you hike above the tree line in early spring.

If you do opt to head to higher elevations with your child, be sure to check with your pediatrician in advance. Depending on the kiddo's age and altitude experience, your doctor may have some specific suggestions for your family.

SAFETY, PREPARATION, AND GEAR

If there is only one piece of advice I can give you before your hike, it is this: Be prepared! That is the motto of every parent ever, and for good reason. If you plan accordingly and pack everything you need, there are very few instances where you will be caught in a bind . . . like that one time I forgot diapers.

The Ten Essentials

First and foremost, always pack the Ten Essentials. The Ten Essentials were a concept originally designed in the 1930s by The Mountaineers, a Seattle-based group of climbers and outdoor enthusiasts. In this original list, they included the ten items they felt any hiker would need to handle an emergency situation and safely spend a night or two outside. Since then, the original ten items have morphed into a systems-based list, but the ideology is the same. Theoretically, you will carry these systems with you on every hike, regardless of whether it is a multiday backpacking trip or a daylong hike. They are as follows:

1. *Navigation (map and compass):* Be sure to always bring a topographic map with you on any trip, as well as a compass. Pro tip: While it's great to have these items in your backpack, it is even more important that you know how to use them! Store the map in a ziplock bag or laminate it to ensure it doesn't get wet or destroyed. With modern technology, many hikers opt to carry GPS devices or even apps on their phone. While these are helpful and can be very useful, technology never replaces the tried-and-true map and compass. Gadgets break or quit or lose battery charge, but a map and compass will always work.

2. *Sun protection (sunglasses and sunscreen):* A sunburn can ruin any trip, so always take the necessary precautions. Wear a hat to protect your face as well as sunglasses to cover your eyes. Never forget sunscreen and lip balm with SPF, either.

3. *Insulation (extra clothing):* Be sure to always have an extra layer or two in case of emergency. Perhaps you take an accidental digger into a stream while hopping across some slippery rocks? Or maybe your daughter poops her pants three times in one mile? You'll be psyched you brought extra clothing to keep everyone (and everything) in check.

4. *Illumination (headlamp or flashlight):* It's rare for a hiker or backpacker to bring a flashlight, but headlamps can be very useful. If your hike goes entirely sideways, it is always possible that you will conclude it in the dark. If this happens, a hands-free light will be absolutely critical. Also, cold weather can zap batteries, so make sure you bring an extra set with you on every trip.

5. *First aid supplies:* Always, always bring medical supplies with you on every trip! And no, we're not simply talking about a box of adhesive bandages. Injuries happen on the trail, and if your partner sprains her ankle while you are trekking 7 miles from the trailhead, you will be very thankful for the splint. Additionally, be sure to bring the supplies that specifically apply to your babe. If you are hiking with a kiddo in diapers, diaper cream is always a good idea since kid carriers combine with heat to create wicked diaper rash. And don't forget the wipes!

6. *Fire (matches or lighter):* Not only will some sort of flame be helpful when it comes time to cook dinner, but these tools are useful if you need to start an emergency fire. These days, most hikers opt for lighters over matches. Whichever you prefer, bring a backup in case your Plan A doesn't work out. Additionally, consider bringing a fire starter with you on every trip. These can be made at home (dryer lint or cotton balls smeared with petroleum jelly are popular choices) and weigh next to nothing, so there is no reason not to carry a few.

7. *Repair kit and tools:* Your dog will pop your sleeping pad one time while winter camping and you will learn your lesson. (Could have happened to anyone . . .) Make sure you pack the basic repair tools on every trip so you can fix any gear emergencies that crop up.

8. *Nutrition (extra food):* Always pack extra food, regardless of how long you will be on the trail. If you are planning on a simple day hike, bring an extra day's worth of calories. If you know you'll be out there for a few nights, plan on more extra food. Regardless of what you choose, be sure the food keeps over time and doesn't require cooking. After all, your emergency situation may mean a stove isn't available. And don't forget child-specific snacks, especially if your kid is not old enough to pack their own. Now that our daughter is three, we like fruit snacks because they work really well as perfectly timed bribery to encourage forward progress on the trail.

9. *Hydration (extra water):* Water is heavy (1 liter weighs roughly 2 pounds), but that doesn't mean you should skimp. Always pack extra to account for emergencies, and be sure to bring some type of filter or purification system so you can clean more if needed (and if water is available). If your child is too young to manage water bottles or bladders on his own, don't forget a sippy cup.

10. *Emergency shelter:* No one wants to sleep in a blizzard during an unplanned night out, but these things occasionally happen. And if they do, you want to ensure you are as safe and protected as possible. Bring an emergency shelter like a small bivvy, tarp, or reflective blanket. Each option weighs only a few ounces but provides copious amounts of mental support.

Be Bear Smart

Many of the hikes featured in this book run through bear country. After all, bears are everywhere! For the most part, these trails stay in black bear country, but brown bears (commonly referred to as grizzly bears) do live in states like Montana and Idaho. It is a great idea to be prepared for either four-legged beast.

Grizzly Bear vs. Black Bear: What's the Difference?

Black bears are the gentle giants of the bear world and can be found in all but ten of the lower forty-eight states. While black bears may appear just as fierce and intimidating as grizzly bears, it is better to think of them as playful cousins. They are much smaller than brown bears and are likely more concerned about finding your bag of food than finding you. Black bears are very smart and can climb trees, making them an annoying menace when it comes to food storage and caching. In fact, these bears are so intelligent that their problem-solving skills vetoed bear bags in favor of bear canisters in popular areas of California and New England; they decoded the bear bag!

Grizzly bears are scarier than black bears thanks to their aggressive personality. You can identify a grizzly thanks to the hump on its back, indicating you are not looking at a black bear. While you certainly don't want to run into a grizzly while hiking, bears truly do not want anything to do with you and will usually only attack if provoked.

Food Storage in Bear Country

Keeping your food on lockdown is the best way to prevent bear interference on your trip. Many bear-heavy areas like Yosemite National Park require bear-resistant storage such as canisters or bear bags. If you opt for a bear bag, be sure you know and understand the guidelines for where to hang the bag and the appropriate distance from camp. Likewise, if you use a bear canister, be sure you know the guidelines for where to stash your canister overnight.

Moreover, always be cognizant of your camp kitchen while backpacking in bear country. Never, ever cook inside your tent as the wafting smell of food may linger on your equipment and invite an unwelcome guest inside during the night. Instead, keep your sleeping location, your camp kitchen, and your food storage location as three distinctly separate areas, creating a triangle of sorts. While this isn't foolproof, it's an effective method to spread out the smell of human food and minimize the likelihood of a bear entering camp while you are sleeping.

If you are day hiking, you still need to be aware of food storage. Believe it or not, bears have been known to gain access to locked vehicles parked at trailheads, all because they smelled a candy bar in the backseat. If you are hiking in bear country, be sure to transfer any and all food from your car to the food-storage lockers included in the parking lot.

Leave No Trace

Leave No Trace (LNT) is the de facto set of outdoor ethics to promote conservation and preservation in the backcountry, as well as minimize the human impact on our green spaces. The bedrock of this sustainability program is a list of seven guiding principles:

1. *Plan ahead and prepare:* Proper planning for any trip ensures you will leave as minimal of an impact as possible. Know and understand high-usage times and avoid them. Research area-specific details so that you can better avoid causing further harm. For example, vegetation in high-alpine zones takes 50–100 years to recover, so understanding this ahead of time may help you be more cautious in your actions.

2. *Travel and camp on a durable surface:* Good campsites are found, not made. Always try to pitch your tent on gravel, hard-packed dirt, rocks, or other sturdy surfaces as opposed to marsh or delicate grasses. Additionally, be sure to always camp at least 200 feet away from lakes and streams to minimize your influence on the aquatic plant life and wildlife.

3. *Dispose of waste properly:* Many people dislike speaking about bathroom behavior but it's easily one of the most discussed topics in the outdoors. We are all human, which means we certainly need to poop while on the trail. If this happens, it's no big deal, but follow the LNT-designed guidelines: Dig a cat hole at least 6–8 inches deep and 200 feet away from water. Then, bury your poop in the hole, ensuring you properly cover it afterwards. And as for trash and litter? Pack it in, pack it out. And yes, this goes for diapers and wipes, too.

4. *Minimize campfire impacts:* As synonymous as fires have become with camping, they are rarely a good idea since they cause lasting impacts to the environment and, especially, damage vegetation that takes years to recover. If you are camping in a dispersed area with a designated fire ring, keep it small and use only small sticks that are snapped by hand. Be sure the fire is out completely before leaving it unattended.

5. *Leave what you find:* Remember in kindergarten when we all learned to look but not touch? That same principle applies to the wilderness. If you happen upon ancient artifacts or historic structures, check 'em out, but let them be without altering or taking them. Likewise, don't create new structures, build trenches, or otherwise change the experience. Think about what the area looked like when you arrived, and then aim to leave it the same *or better* for the next person. This can be tricky when hiking with toddlers who want to TOUCH EVERYTHING, but try your best to ensure your child doesn't do any permanent damage.

6. *Respect wildlife:* In recent years, the USA has seen an increase in human involvement with wildlife. Just because the mountain goats or deer come up to your campsite does not mean they are domestic; they are still wild animals. Never

feed, follow, or approach these animals, and certainly try not to get too close. This is for you both your safety and the animals' welfare.

7. *Be considerate of other visitors:* We all hit the trail to gain a wilderness experience full of beauty and solitude. To that end, try your best to preserve that same experience for others. Don't blast your music while hiking or yell and shout late at night while camping close to others. Basically, mind your manners so everyone can equally enjoy their time outside.

Additionally, the twenty-first century has brought about a wave of new Leave No Trace discussions revolving around social media. Thanks to the power of platforms like Instagram and Facebook, millions of users are geotagging specific locations while showcasing stunning scenery. In turn, hundreds of thousands of new visitors are heading to that specific location to see the real-life version of what they enjoyed in the photo. As a result, heavily photographed locations are becoming overrun and abused.

Leave No Trace recently released a brief list of suggested social media guidelines for the digital era. They included the following tips:

1. *Tag thoughtfully:* If you opt to geotag a specific location, try to include appropriate Leave No Trace information. This will empower people to take care of these wild spaces and encourage future learning.

2. *Be mindful of what your images portray:* So frequently, popular social media influencers showcase photos of picturesque scenes, such as a colorful tent pitched below a towering peak. But there is one problem: That tent is pitched smack next to a body of water, and the account just subconsciously shared that with thousands of followers. Be aware of the images you share on your social media account to encourage your followers to conserve the wilderness just as you do.

3. *Give back to places you love:* Get involved with volunteer projects to help give back to your favorite trails. These trails won't maintain themselves!

4. *Encourage and inspire Leave No Trace in your social media posts:* Regardless of whether you have 100 followers or 100,000, encourage them to take care of green spaces too.

HIKING TIPS AND SUGGESTIONS

There are two ways to look at this. First, I could go off the rails and detail all of the necessary gear and equipment that will make your adventure more comfortable and easier. We could talk about backpacks and hiking shoes, tents and sleeping bags. Or, I could remind you of the old adage: Hike your own hike. But what does that really mean?

So frequently, I think newcomers to hiking get caught up in all of the details and fancy-sounding words. If you walk into any outdoor goods store, you will be bombarded with words like *denier* and *ultralight* and *shank* and *outsole*. And if you are already well-versed in outdoor gear, that is great. These words are all important and make sense—once you are prepared to deal with them. But if they are as familiar to you as a foreign language, you are likely to feel overwhelmed. And I would hate for that to happen.

The spirit of this book lies with the women featured. Some of them are hardcore, robust athletes while others are outdoor inspirations who are passionate about wild spaces. Neither is right or wrong and you have to decide which trail works best for you. If you want to challenge yourself, check out the hikes detailed by Ilana Jesse, Cherine Gibbons, or Christina McEvoy. There is no shortage of burning lungs and heavy backpacks on those trails. Or, if you are just beginning and/or want a mellow day filled with just a touch of Mother Nature, take a look at the trails chosen by Jennifer Pharr Davis, Dineo Dowd, or Jenny Taylor. These women opted for these particular hikes especially for their inclusive nature and welcome attitude toward everyone, regardless of abilities.

So again, I say: Hike your own hike and do whatever is best for your family on that particular day. That is up to you to decide.

PHOTOGRAPHY TIPS AND SUGGESTIONS

It does not matter whether you cart an elaborate camera with multiple lenses or a basic smartphone; you will certainly want to snap more than a few photos while on your hike. In doing so, you will accomplish the first requirement of great photography: getting out there. But once there, how can you ensure that you will shoot the best possible photos? Here are a few tips from Will Rochfort, my husband and the published photographer responsible for the cover of this book.

1. *Always have your camera accessible.* If it is a hassle to find it inside your backpack, you are less likely to take the time to shoot photos. Instead, find a system that works for you. If using a smartphone, store it in your pants pocket or in the waist belt pocket on your backpack. If you are using a larger camera, come up with a carrying method. For smaller point-and-shoots, a small camera case looped through the sternum strap on your backpack works very well. For a larger DSLR camera, a front-carry pack provides the same accessibility while acting as a counterbalance to your backpack.

2. *Focus on the light.* Dramatic subjects can look boring in flat light while mediocre subjects can appear downright dazzling with a beautiful evening glow. Focus your photography on the best capture of the light. Often this means shooting

in the early morning or evening; often, the least flattering light is the overhead sunshine of midday.

3. *Carry a tripod.* Yes, this is extra weight, but your photos will thank you! It doesn't need to be fancy; a light, compact tripod will work. Find an option that you are willing to carry since stabilizing your camera may be crucial to many of your desired photos.

4. *Don't forget the extras.* If you shoot with a DSLR, remember to pack all of the extra equipment like memory cards, batteries, a cloth to clean your lenses, polarizers, and a charger if needed. There is nothing worse than setting up a shot of a stunning backcountry sunset only to realize that your dead battery light is flashing.

5. *Pixels are cheap.* It is a digital era, which means we don't pay to develop every single photo anymore. Snap as many photos as you want; you can sort through and delete the unwanted captures once you return home.

6. *Always grab the memory photos.* As a photographer, it is easy to get caught up in the "perfect" photos: a glorious sunrise, an action hiking shot, or a quick glimpse of the black bear as he wanders through the wildflowers. But don't forget to take those often-cheesy photos with your group smiling at camp or posing by the trailhead sign. They won't feel as glamorous as your other photos, but these are the ones that help preserve your cherished memories. In our family, these classic standing-by-the-sign photos are the absolute best to look at over time.

Map Legend

Municipal

- 101 US Highway
- 92 State Road
- 31 County/Forest/Local Road
- Unpaved Road
- Railroad
- Country Boundary
- State/Province Boundary

Trails

- Featured Trail
- Trail
- Off-trail Route

Symbols

- Bridge
- Building/Point of Interest
- Campground
- Lodging
- Parking
- Peak/Elevation
- Ranger Station
- Restroom
- Ski Area
- Town
- 20 Trailhead

Water Features

- Body of Water
- Glacier
- River/Creek
- Intermittent Stream
- Waterfall
- Spring

Land Management

- National Park/Forest
- Wilderness Area
- State/County Park
- Natural Area
- Indian Reservation

CASSIE ABEL

Proctor Mountain Loop
Sun Valley, Idaho

Cassie Abel is the cofounder and current owner of Wild Rye, an outdoor apparel company designed specifically for female mountain bikers. Born and raised on Vashon Island outside of Seattle, Cassie has a varied career that began with her leaving Washington for school at Colorado College. Post-graduation, she found her way to California's Bay Area for a job in finance while coaching lacrosse at the University of California, Berkeley. But thanks to her love of skiing, she found herself heading to Tahoe every single weekend. Over time, she realized the 6-hour round-trip drive was a waste of valuable hours, so she vowed to move back to the mountains. Eventually, she settled in Sun Valley, Idaho, for what she thought would be her forever job with Smith Optics, but was saddened when the brand relocated their headquarters to Portland, Oregon. Cassie needed to choose between staying in the mountains or following

Cassie Abel and her son, Sawyer MIKE STEMP

her career, and ultimately she opted to stay in Sun Valley where she founded White Cloud Communications, a PR and marketing communications firm. Through that, she reconnected with an old friend in the Bay Area and the two of them began chatting about a female apparel company. In 2016, the duo launched Wild Rye, and by January 2019, Cassie bought out her partner to become the sole owner.

Today, Cassie still lives in Sun Valley with her husband and son Sawyer, who was born in December 2019.

Although usually known for its breathtaking ski slopes, Sun Valley is an all-season outdoorist's dream. Found just outside of town, Proctor Mountain Loop is a moderate hike usually done in a clockwise direction. On a clear day, the hefty elevation gain brings you to sweeping views of the surrounding towns and national forest. You may encounter some wildlife, but the real showstopper of this trail is the wildflowers found rolling along the hills at every turn. After a steep descent, it's a quick drive back into town where a cold post-hike beverage and accompanying grub can easily be found.

Sawyer and Kirby waiting for the hike to begin
Mike Stemp

Nearest town: Sun Valley

Getting there: For visitors entering Sun Valley from Ketchum, take Saddle Road east from Route 75. After a half mile, Saddle Road turns into Dollar Road. Follow Dollar Road for 0.7 mile, and then it turns into Fairway Road. Another 1.7 miles brings you to the end of the road and a small, residential cul-de-sac. Parking is on either side of the road but please be mindful of those who live in the area.

Trailhead: Proctor Mountain Trailhead

GPS: N43 42.726' / W114 20.154'

Fees and permits: No fee or permit required

Trail users: Hikers, trail runners

Elevation gain: 1,610 feet

Length: 4.4 miles (loop)

Approximate hiking time: Half day

Difficulty: Moderate

Seasonal highlights: The hills along this trail are flourishing with wildflowers during peak season (usually mid- to late June). Make sure to do this one early in the morning or later in the evening during summer months, as there is little shade for reprieve.

Managing agency: US Forest Service–Sawtooth National Forest

EXPERIENCING IT

Cassie Abel spent the first 5 months of her son's life chained to the stroller.

When Sawyer was born in late December, Sun Valley was entrenched in the icy blasts of winter, signaling the start of the town's popular ski season. But for the first time in a while, the winter of 2019–20 was not about skiing for Cassie. There wouldn't be much—if any—powder-filled dawn patrols or lofty pillow drops this season. Instead, January found Cassie and her husband operating on minimal sleep and diaper duty.

But as a lifelong athlete, Cassie couldn't handle sitting still indoors all day. She needed to move, to get outside and feel the wintry blasts on her cheeks. So instead of

Cassie showing Kirby a little love MIKE STEMP

grabbing her two planks and ski poles, Cassie bundled Sawyer in a snowsuit and loaded him into the stroller. The duo was taking a walk. It may have been easier to carry her son in a soft front-carry system, but Sawyer wanted none of that. While some babies are quickly lulled to sleep by the warmth of their mama's chest and the sensation of her beating heart, Sawyer felt confined in the front carrier. He didn't enjoy the feeling of being trapped and he let Cassie know he was displeased through uninterrupted hollering and screaming. At times, his complaints hit new octaves of hysteria, completely stressing Cassie out and ruining any semblance of sanity she gleaned from the walks outside. So no, a front carrier was never easier.

The car seat didn't help either. As the novel coronavirus pandemic swept the nation, Cassie and her husband found themselves traveling less and less. As a result, Sawyer developed an equal hatred for his car seat—darn confinement!—because he never needed to be in it. *We don't like what we don't know, right?* Similar to the front carry,

Cassie, all smiles because the hike is going so well! Mike Stemp

FUN FACTS ABOUT SUN VALLEY

Sun Valley, Idaho, is a resort community that boasts a unique blend of European roots in an American environment. For that reason, it's one of the most coveted ski destinations in the United States. But how much do you actually know about Sun Valley? Let's test your skills with four fun facts about the area.

1. Sun Valley was the first ski resort to build a chairlift. Averill Harriman, the mastermind behind Sun Valley, knew he wanted a better way to cart skiers uphill when compared to the beloved rope tows that were popular at the time. He turned to an engineer named James Curran, who had once designed a wire-based system to haul bananas from the docks to the boats in Honduras. James used this technology to create the original single chairs that opened during the 1936–37 ski season.

2. The name "Sun Valley" came from a PR pro in New York City who thought it was an appropriate name for an area that saw more than 250 days of sun per year.

3. It could be argued that Sun Valley has the best lift lines—because there aren't any. The resort's uphill lift capacity on Bald Mountain can move 21,580 skiers per hour yet the hill typically averages 3,500 skiers per day. This results in an uber efficient system with very few people, so you'll never wait around.

4. Not only do celebrities love Sun Valley, but so does Batman. Adam West, the original Batman, lived in the area for decades. To this day, various characters like "Bruce Wayne" and "Batman" still show up in the phone book.

this made car rides excessively stressful, no matter how short the distance. Thankfully, Cassie knew her son enjoyed the stroller, so it was back to the bike path.

Each day, she plopped Sawyer in his infant stroller and they meandered through Sun Valley along the paved trails. It didn't matter if it was overcast and flurrying or sunny and warm; Cassie needed those walks. It gave her time to think about how much life had changed in a few short months, and it also allowed her to see a glimpse of her former self. Walking with the stroller wasn't hiking or biking or skiing, but it was movement and she was grateful for every minute of it. Plus, it made Sawyer happy, which was paramount to Cassie's sanity in those early days. She found herself walking or riding her bike 10 miles down the bike path to see a friend rather than forcing her son into the car seat, simply because it was easier on everyone. It wasn't a perfect

It's not easy to carry a baby but the views from the shoulder make the sweat worth it.
MIKE STEMP

solution, but in her sleep-deprived state, Cassie wasn't looking for perfect. She was looking for survival.

The snowy drifts melted and the warmer temperatures returned to Sun Valley. As spring faded into early summer, Cassie was gifted a new Osprey kid carrier for Sawyer. Based on her past experiences with the front carrier, she didn't have high expectations but still carried the pack home to present to her son. His reaction was *priceless*! Immediately, Sawyer sensed the kid carrier was for him and a wide smile spread across his face. He gestured toward the backpack, requesting that his mother put him inside. She did and his joy was palpable. For the remainder of the day, Cassie and her husband took turns carrying their son around the house in his new favorite ride.

But the next day was the real test. Cassie decided to hit the trail, venturing to the local favorite, Proctor Mountain Loop. Sawyer had loved the backpack at home, but she had no idea whether he would feel equally enthused on the hike.

Vivid yellow arrowleaf balsamroot and purple and pink lupine dotted the meadows, creating a colorful wildflower explosion along the horizon as Cassie shouldered the

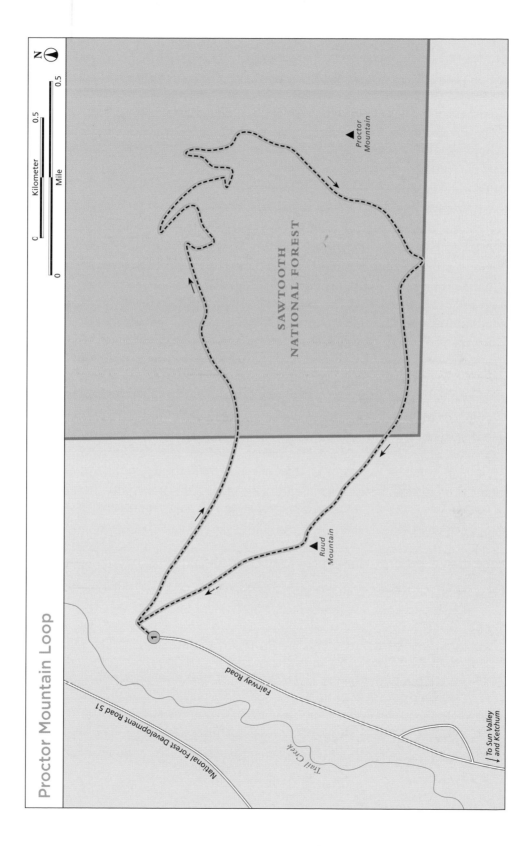

Proctor Mountain Loop

Osprey. She headed up the trail, anticipating the squawking that never came. As she and her husband waded through the cornucopia of flowers and continued climbing up toward the route's high point, she realized Sawyer was enjoying himself. By the time the family reached the grassy saddle, Cassie felt a newfound freedom.

She scanned the horizon, soaking in the views of the Sun Valley ski area still speckled up high with late-season snow. Behind her, Sawyer contentedly babbled from his perch in the Osprey, wiggling from side to side while snot dripped from his nose. He could move in his carrier, so he was happy.

For the price of a child carrier, Cassie had just gotten a piece of her life back.

THE HIKE

Begin your hike up one of two paths from the parking area along Fairway Road. The two trails converge at the start of the Proctor Mountain Loop trailhead. Although this loop trail can be hiked either direction, it is recommended to go clockwise. As the trail winds its way up, the path becomes narrower and traverses through grassy knolls and aspen groves. During midsummer, the hills are filled with hundreds of wildflowers that are just too beautiful to ignore. As you begin to climb the steep set of switchbacks, the scenery changes to evergreens, which gives a nice reprieve from the hot sun. After about a mile and a half, the path meets up with the Aspen Loop, but make sure to continue on to Proctor/Rudd Mountain Loop. At this point, the remainder of the trail has little to no shade, so be aware of the time of day you start the hike—it could be a scorcher! The trail heads up to the top of the valley and tops out just shy of Proctor Mountain. At mile 3, make sure to keep an eye out for a sharp right turn off the main path toward a grassy knoll. The trail eventually plunges down the ridge toward Ruud Mountain where the old Ruud Mountain chairlift still stands. Finally, the trail meets back up at the trailhead where you'll take one of the two paths back to your car.

MILES AND DIRECTIONS

0.0 Begin hiking by taking one of two paths on the east side of Fairway Road and continue onto Proctor Mountain Loop trail.

0.8 Start the steep ascent of switchbacks.

1.6 Meet up with Aspen Loop. Take a right to continue on Proctor/Rudd Mountain Loop.

2.5 Reach the high point of the trail at 7,632 feet on the northwestern ridge of Proctor Mountain.

2.9 Abrupt right off the "main" trail toward a grassy knoll.

3.8 The site of the old Ruud Mountain chairlift.

4.4 Arrive back where you started.

MELODY BUCK FORSYTH

Tower Bridge Trail
Bryce Canyon National Park, Utah

Based in Salt Lake City, Utah, Melody Buck Forsyth has worked as a labor-and-delivery nurse for the past 19 years. This 45-year-old mother is passionate about her career and truly loves bringing new life into the world. She can't imagine doing anything else—even while working graveyard shifts from 7 p.m. to 7 a.m.

Melody is also an activist for children with Down syndrome around the country. As a lifelong hiker, Melody admits that she feared her outdoor adventures were numbered when she found out her fourth child, Ruby, would be born with Down syndrome. Instead, she learned the best was yet to come and continued to find ways to hit the trail with Ruby (4), Samuel (10), Logan (13), Angelina (19), and her husband, Victor. Today, Melody uses the power of social media to both educate the general public and crush stereotypes about children with Down syndrome.

Melody Buck Forsyth carrying her daughter Ruby MELODY BUCK FORSYTH

A good hike for those visiting Bryce Canyon National Park, the trail to Tower Bridge can be done as an out-and-back hike or combined with the Fairyland Loop for a longer day of hiking. This top-down trail brings you away from the crowds circling the park loop to the observation points and into the heart of the park. On top of seeing Tower Bridge, you'll also be granted majestic views of the hoodoos, arches, and towering sandstone walls that make Bryce Canyon so marvelous. If you want to add some distance to your hike, you can always continue on the Fairyland Loop Trail for a full, adventurous day of hiking.

Nearest town: Bryce

Getting there: For visitors entering from the north, take I-15 south to exit 95. Go east on Route 20 for 20 miles and then take a right to head south on US 89 for 17 miles. Turn left onto Route 12 east for 13 miles, then head south on Route 63 for 4 miles. Parking is at the Sunrise Observation Point.

Trailhead: Rim Trailhead

GPS: N37 37.896' / W112 09.882'

Fees and permits: Hikers and other day users need a National Park Day Pass ($35 per car)

Trail users: Hikers, trail runners

Elevation gain: 826 feet

Length: 3.4 miles (out-and-back)

Approximate hiking time: Half day

Difficulty: Moderate

Seasonal highlights: Due to its desert environment, the best time to visit Tower Bridge is in the spring or fall when the daytime temperatures are within a pleasant range. That said, the best time of day to take in the views from this trail is at sunrise, just like the parking lot's name suggests.

Managing agency: National Park Service–Bryce Canyon National Park

EXPERIENCING IT

Ruby was only 2 years old when Melody heard the first comment.

Per usual, Ruby sat perched in the kid carrier on Melody's back as the duo hiked up the Red Pine Trail in Little Cottonwood Canyon outside of Salt Lake. Adamant

The Forsyth family (L-R): Angelina, Victor, Samuel, and Logan MELODY BUCK FORSYTH

that her daughter enjoy the fresh air and sunshine afforded to the rest of her children, Melody had already grown accustomed to hiking with a small human on her back. She moved slower and her shoulders hurt, but those discomforts were a small price to pay for her daughter's happiness. She smiled to herself as she heard Ruby giggling in the backpack, marveling at the leaves dancing along the tree branches and the fluffy clouds slowly trailing through the azure skyline. It was a good day.

But a man hiking toward the mother-daughter twosome pulled Melody out of her reverie. She lifted her head in acknowledgment as they passed by, and he smiled in return before saying, "That's quite a burden you're carrying there."

Seven words. While small in stature, those seven words hit Melody like a sucker punch to the stomach. How dare anyone consider her daughter a burden? She kept hiking, carefully considering his statement while dissecting it for potential meaning. As her emotions simmered just below boiling, she acknowledged the truth: Many people still consider special needs children to be problematic or more work. In that moment, Melody made a promise to herself: She would always make sure that Ruby knew she was loved and wanted and never, ever considered a burden.

"I don't consider her one more thing I have to do," Melody says. "Even if I have to carry her, I love getting to share those experiences."

Fast forward 3 years and Melody still remembers the hiker's words in the mountains and lives by her promise to Ruby. Ruby comes along on every single hike, even now that she weighs nearly 45 pounds. So when Logan's birthday rolled around and the family opted to spend his twelfth celebration at Bryce Canyon National Park, they loaded up the kid carrier for the family road trip and headed to canyon country.

Melody and Ruby are both all-smiles! MELODY BUCK FORSYTH

Once in Bryce Canyon, the Forsyth family settled on the Tower Bridge Trail. While not the easiest trek in the park, Tower Bridge was a great option for everyone since the route immediately descends into the red earth, offering an easy start from the parking lot. Logan practically danced down the path, reveling in his birthday adventure while admiring the vivid orange hoodoos offset with creamy-white striations as they stood in stark contrast to the vivid blue sky in the background. For her part, Angelina trailed at the back of the pack, peppering her parents with teenage complaints about the warm weather and lack of shade.

At the base of the canyon, the family regrouped for a lunch break while Melody changed Ruby's diaper. After all, what was a Forsyth adventure on the trail without a diaper blowout?! Once the kids had full bellies and rested legs, the clan began their 800-foot ascent back to the parking lot.

Of course, things got interesting.

The day wasn't terribly warm—it was in the low 80s, which is minor in Utah's desert country—and Melody had previously dismissed Angelina's complaints as the typical teenage grievances. But as she began climbing out of the canyon floor, Melody felt the effects of the heat herself. She slowly moved upward, carefully placing one foot in front of the other while ensuring Ruby's safety in the kid carrier. But her pace slowed even further and she felt a rush of adrenaline surge through her body. She stopped moving and braced herself as a dull ringing filled her ears. As the surrounding sounds disappeared and she heard only silence, she sank to the ground. "I'm going down," she faintly called to her husband before settling onto the colorful earth.

There she was, sitting in the middle of the trail with Ruby still perched on her back. White stars sprinkled her eyesight but her vision returned as she rested her body in the warm Utah sun. After jogging back, Melody's husband offered her electrolytes and cool water that internally awakened her senses. But still, she knew better. With a mile

Welcome to Bryce
Canyon National Park
WILL ROCHFORT

The hoodoos of Bryce Canyon are especially memorable on a bluebird day. Will Rochfort

A HOODOO ORIGIN STORY

Bryce Canyon National Park is nationally known for its distinctly colorful orange-and-white hoodoos, or tall and thin spires of rock. Visitors flock from all over the country just to see these unique formations. Many assume the hoodoos were formed by wind, but that isn't the case in Bryce Canyon. Instead, these mythical spires were created by the magical erosive powers of water, ice, and gravity.

Although the high point of Bryce Canyon National Park now sits at an impressive 9,105 feet, the entire park once lived at sea level on the Colorado Plateau. However, around 100 million years ago, the Farallon tectonic plate began to subduct beneath the North American plate, driving the Colorado Plateau up to its current elevation. At its new height, the plateau was exposed to harsher weather conditions like wind, rain, and ice. Over time, water seeped into small cracks and fissures in the rock, and when the temperatures dropped, the moisture froze and turned into ice. As it did, the ice expanded and gradually broke the rock apart in varying ways. First, the stone would break into a solid wall; then, a window-like hole would appear. Eventually, the rock was carved into the impressive spires we see today.

of climbing left until they arrived back at the parking lot, Melody could not carry Ruby any farther.

In that moment, she realized she was carting an additional burden: the weight of her promise to Ruby. Somewhere along the way, her vow became a shield of armor and Melody realized that asking for help was not a sign of weakness. In her effort to be a pillar of strength for her daughter, Melody had forgotten one key lesson: Even the mighty need support.

"Everyone always tells me, 'Oh, you're so strong!' when they see me carrying Ruby and I think that makes it even harder for me to ask for help," Melody says.

She relinquished the kid carrier, allowing her husband to transfer it from her body to his. Melody sat in the dirt and watched as he began moving upward, carrying his daughter while she babbled and fluffed his hair with her little hands. He laughed in amusement and bounced a little bit, causing Ruby to erupt in a new wave of giggles as her body briefly defied gravity. That's when Melody realized: She needed to make space for his parental enjoyment, too.

For so long, carrying Ruby on the trail was Melody's special bond with her daughter. It began as a promise but gradually morphed into a pledge deeper than surface words. In her effort to support Ruby, Melody inadvertently shut others out of the relationship.

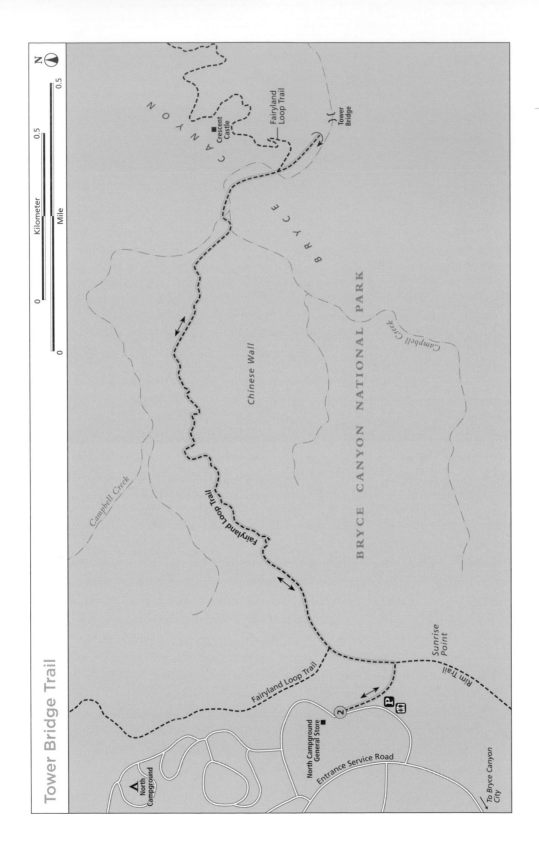

"It's not all about me," she says. "I was thinking a lot about Ruby but not a lot about other people and I realized I need to give my husband those opportunities too."

Her husband carried Ruby up the rest of the trail, scampering and laughing with his daughter for the remainder of the afternoon. Melody trailed behind, smiling to herself as she watched her family play in the colorful Utah desert.

Melody's husband, Victor, carries Ruby up the trail.
MELODY BUCK FORSYTH

THE HIKE

Begin your hike at the Rim Trailhead located at the parking lot for Sunrise Observation Point within Bryce Canyon National Park. You'll soon join with the Fairyland Loop Trail (an 8-mile hike around Bryce Canyon National Park that highlights the region's grandeur) where you'll get sweeping views of the canyon and its trademark red rock hoodoos. For that matter, the first mile of the trail boasts big views of the Chinese Wall and Sinking Ship formations. As the trail descends further into the canyon, you'll pass the famous bristlecone pines that are scattered throughout the area. As you continue down, eventually the trail levels off and you'll cross a creek bed. Afterwards, the trail forks and you'll stay to the right and follow signs for Tower Bridge. You'll reach another creek bed with Tower Bridge above. Snap your photos here! After shooting your best photo, head a little farther up to get closer to the geological phenomenon. Return the way you came to get back to the trailhead.

MILES AND DIRECTIONS

0.0 Begin hiking at the Rim Trailhead at the Sunrise Observation Point.

0.3 Link up with the Fairyland Loop Trail.

0.8 Start to see a sharp contrast to the spectacular rock formations.

1.5 First creek bed crossing (creek may be running or not depending on the season).

1.6 Trail forks; keep right toward signs for Tower Bridge; and a second creek bed crossing.

1.7 Tower Bridge.

3.4 Arrive back at the trailhead.

LARA DORMAN

Iceberg Lake
Glacier National Park, Montana

Born and raised in Southern California, Lara Dorman moved to Montana for college to be closer to outdoor recreation. After university, she joined the United States Army

Lara Dorman (top left) with her wife, Deb, and their two children, Isabelle and Isaac
LARA DORMAN

(and subsequently the National Guard) where she spent 22 years serving her country in Germany and the USA. Before retirement, she ran the Equal Opportunity Training Program in Montana, a region that did not have the best track record on the subject. However, in the late 2000s, the 1993 policy of "Don't Ask, Don't Tell" (DADT) once again dominated the headlines as various legal appeals challenged the military directive. Originally introduced by the Clinton administration, DADT prohibited military personnel from harassing or discriminating against gay or bisexual service members. But it also prohibited people who "demonstrate a propensity or intent to engage in homosexual acts" from serving in the armed forces, supposedly because their presence would "create an unacceptable risk to the high standards of morale, good order, and discipline." Lara was up for a promotion to major at the time, but felt uncomfortable remaining in the military since she knew her relationship with her now-wife was public and present in her community. As a result, she retired as a captain in 2010.

Today, she now works as a part-time realtor and part-time freelance travel writer. She is married to her wife, Deb, and they have two children: Isabelle (13) and Isaac (12). The family lives in Missoula, Montana, but frequently travels due to Deb's work with her road construction company.

Enjoyed as a moderate day hike, Iceberg Lake is one of the more popular trails within Glacier National Park even with its remote location. Hikers are blessed with an abundance of wildflowers and plenty of wildlife viewing along the trail. Spring thaw usually brings hungry grizzly bears to the area, so be on the lookout, make lots of noise, and check the trail status prior to your trip since it's often closed due to bear activity. Although Iceberg Lake is considered a longer hike, it has minimal elevation gain, making it a trail for most hikers.

Nearest town: Babb

Getting there: For visitors entering from the south on US 89, take a left on Route 3 for 7.5 miles until you reach the entrance to Glacier National Park. Continue on Route 3 for 4.5 miles until you reach Swiftcurrent Motor Inn. There is a small parking area behind the cabins, but if it's full, you'll have to park in front of the inn.

Trailhead: Iceberg Lake/Ptarmigan Trailhead

GPS: N48 47.976' / W113 40.752'

Fees and permits: Day users will need an America the Beautiful Interagency Pass ($80 per year) or a Glacier National Park day pass ($35 per vehicle).

Trail users: Hikers, trail runners

Elevation gain: 1,348 feet

Length: 9.8 miles (out-and-back)

Approximate hiking time: Full day

Difficulty: Moderate

Seasonal highlights: Due to its northern location, be on the lookout during spring thaw as you will be in prime bear and moose habitat. Never approach wildlife and remember to follow the Leave No Trace principles.

Managing agency: National Park Service–Glacier National Park

EXPERIENCING IT

Isabelle and Isaac started big from a small age. Thanks to their proximity to Glacier National Park (Missoula is merely two hours from the boundary line), Lara Dorman and her children frequently wandered into the park for some trail therapy beginning when the kids were just babies. Lara and Deb foisted their son and daughter into kid carriers, shouldering the wiggly weight with joy since it meant they could spend their Saturdays exploring some of the most iconic trails in the country. As the babes grew into toddlers and then young kids, they graduated from kid carriers to full-blown hiking. But as much as Lara loved being outside herself, she never wanted to push her children. Instead, she encouraged them to accomplish whatever distance possible within the realm of enjoyment. This way, she figured, she would develop their love of hiking at an early age so they could tackle grander challenges when they were older.

By the time the summer of 2019 rolled around, Lara had a pair of veteran preteen hikers. One warm summer morning, the trio opted to head to Ptarmigan Falls, a 5-mile round-trip hike in the park that

Isaac trekking along the approach to Iceberg Lake Lara Dorman

boasted minimal elevation gain and commanding views of the inimitable 8,851-foot Mt. Grinnell. While the trail doesn't navigate too closely to the 200-foot series of cascades, Ptarmigan felt like a safe bet for Lara and her children alike.

But as Lara steered their car into the trailhead, she immediately noticed that the fifteen-space parking lot was full and park rangers were directing traffic to another location a mile down the road. She obliged, maneuvering her car to the new space, but couldn't help but hear Isaac grumbling in the backseat. "Mo-om! Now we have to add another mile each way onto the hike!" he complained.

EVERYTHING YOU NEED TO KNOW ABOUT GLACIER NATIONAL PARK'S GLACIERS

Glacier National Park is situated in northern Montana, smack on the Canada–US border. Designated a national park in 1910, Glacier was the United States' tenth national park. While you may already know about the glaciers that carved the mountains in the park, did you know these fun facts?

1. *The namesake glaciers are melting.* When the park received its designation more than 100 years ago, there were approximately 150 glaciers over 25 acres in size. Thanks to climate change, that number has shrunk to 26 and scientists estimate that all of the glaciers will be gone by 2030.

2. *Glacier is part of the world's first-ever International Peace Park.* Glacier sits just over the international boundary from Canada's Waterton Lakes National Park. The two countries decided that the upper Waterton Valley shouldn't be split between two countries, so the nations joined together in 1932 as a gesture of goodwill.

3. *Mountain goats are a big deal.* You won't hike a single trail without encountering one of these friendly fellows on the hillside. As a result, these goats are the official symbol of the entire park.

4. *The ecosystem hasn't changed in over a hundred years.* Home to more than seventy-one species of mammals, the park's ecosystem has remained virtually intact and unbothered since its early days when Europeans first saw it. At present, woodland caribou and bison are the only animals to no longer wander this part of Montana.

5. *Human evidence dates back over 12,000 years.* Archaeologists have discovered signs of human occupation that date back to the retreat of the Ice Age glaciers. These people were likely ancestors to the Blackfeet and Kootenai Native people who still live in the area today.

"That's okay!" Lara cheerfully exclaimed with a classic mother response. "It might be a parking lot but we're in Glacier so it's still beautiful terrain!"

Ptarmigan Falls lives in the Many Glacier area, a region ripe with grizzly bears. In particular, the first mile of terrain is riddled with the magnificent beasts, and this day was no different. Lara, Isaac, and Isabelle had barely hiked 5 minutes when the family spotted two brown bears foraging on the hillside. Despite their massive size, the bears felt friendly as they virtually ignored the hikers in favor of the delectable greenery at their feet. The grizzlies crunched and munched as Lara and the kids kept moving.

The wildlife show continued all the way to the waterfalls. After the bears, the family spotted a handful of deer and a few mountain goats, as is typical in Glacier. By the time they all reached Ptarmigan Falls, everyone was giddy with such a successful outing. But as the trio sat in the shade and ate their sandwiches, Lara overheard another family talking about Iceberg Lake.

While she and the kids had only planned on voyaging to Ptarmigan and back, the rest of the surrounding hikers were tackling the entire 10-mile journey to Iceberg Lake, using the waterfalls as a brief respite before continuing on the trail. Lara hadn't even considered that option at home because double-digit mileage sounded like way too much of a challenging proposition for her children. But as she sat on the rock and heard the others lauding its glistening waters and sparkling scenery, she made a game-time decision.

Isabelle excitedly hiking closer to the glacier-blue waters Lara Dorman

"Alright, you two! Change of plans. We're hiking to Iceberg," Lara stated before grabbing her gear and standing up.

"Mo-om!" Isaac moaned. "That's so much farther! You said we were only going to Ptarmigan!"

But Lara was having none of it. After years of carefully preparing diaper packages and counting out enough calories and gear for her young children to ensure they survived the hikes in comfort, she was ready for her family to once again find spontaneity on the trail. They were old enough and she knew they were strong enough. Today was going to be an adventure.

Isabelle acquiesced first, and before long, Isaac fell into step. But it didn't take long for the family to shake off the change in plans and marvel in the excitement at what was to come. Isaac continued grumbling but his complaints grew further and further apart as they hiked higher and higher. By the time everyone reached the jewel waters of Iceberg, the past discomfort was a distant memory.

A massive cirque of imposing peaks looped around the lake while rising more than 3,000 feet above the icy waters. Thanks to its naturally shaded state, minimal sunlight dappled the frosty waters so floating pockets of ice and snow skipped across the surface and a larger iceberg bobbed in the center of the lake. A few brave hikers jumped into the chilly waters, gasping for air as the icy-tinged liquid touched their

Soaking in the views at Iceberg Lake LARA DORMAN

skin. Isaac and Isabelle couldn't go in (the family didn't grab lifejackets for their impromptu excursion), so instead, Lara and the kids explored the high-alpine meadows skirting the shoreline and removed their hiking boots to dip their sweaty feet in the cool waters. While watching the dancing pool ripple away from their toes, Isaac looked at his mom and smiled. "Next time, I want to swim to the iceberg," he said.

Lara smiled back, not only because she knew there *would* be a next time, but also because she knew there *could* be another one. In that moment, she realized Iceberg

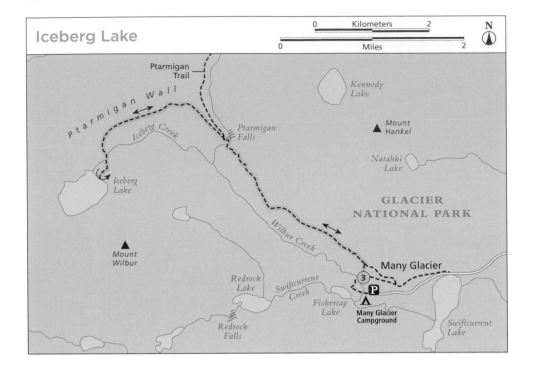

Iceberg Lake

was a turning point for her family. The hike wasn't a cataclysmic event that changed the trajectory of her life, but this beautiful day was symbolic of the greater picture. Isaac and Isabelle were growing up and all those years of gentle encouragement and copious snack breaks on the trail were behind them. Now, they had years filled with spontaneous decisions ahead, and they were strong children who enjoyed being the drivers of the adventure—not just the passengers. It was bittersweet, of course, to realize her babies were no longer babies, but there was power in knowing that grander things lay ahead.

"Let's keep going," Lara said.

THE HIKE

Begin your hike at the Iceberg Lake/Ptarmigan Trailhead just behind the Swiftcurrent Motor Inn. The first part of the hike offers grand views in its open vista (where making noise to ward off any wildlife in the area will suit you well) but soon turns to more densely forested terrain. When you emerge from the forest, you'll enter a small clearing where you can see Ptarmigan Falls, although it's not the most memorable scene since the steep terrain doesn't allow for a full view. You will then meander through more forest and more clearings until you reach a point where you can see the cirque with Iceberg Lake at its base. Ptarmigan Wall (the thin rock face separating the two valleys) can be seen slightly after that. Soon enough, you will cross Iceberg Creek along a foot bridge and be close to your destination. It may be crowded at the trail outlet but skirt around either side of the lake for some solitude.

MILES AND DIRECTIONS

0.0 Begin hiking at the Iceberg Lake/Ptarmigan Trailhead near the Swift-current Motor Inn.

0.1 Take the short (but steep!) connector trail that leads to Ptarmigan Trail. Turn left when you reach that junction.

1.7 Enter a densely forested area.

2.5 Reach a small clearing for the best view of Ptarmigan Falls.

2.6 Reach the Ptarmigan Trail/Iceberg Lake Trail junction. Keep left at the fork.

3.1 The trail opens up to another small clearing where you can see the destination in front of you.

4.3 Cross Iceberg Creek along a foot bridge.

4.9 Iceberg Lake. Retrace your steps.

9.8 Arrive back at the trailhead.

4

DINEO DOWD
Parfrey's Glen
Merrimac, Wisconsin

Dineo Dowd with her daughter, Armani DINEO DOWD

Dineo Dowd is a full-time mother and children's book author who hails from South Africa. After moving to Utah in 2012, Dineo began to explore the outdoors, but it wasn't until she gave birth to her daughter Armani (age 5) that she began noticing the lack of diversity in outdoor-based children's books. She wanted to create wilderness adventure stories where Armani could see characters who looked like her. To date, Dineo has published four children's books: *The Dowd's Adventure: Summer Camping*, *Spring Hike*, *Adventure Day*, and *Sunset Hike*.

Dineo is also a board member for the nonprofit Hike it Baby, a 501(c)(3) organization that aims to connect families to nature. Previous to her role on the board of directors, Dineo was a branch ambassador, helping to lead community members on hikes with their children. Presently, Dineo is married and lives with her husband and daughter in Madison, Wisconsin.

Likely considered the most visited state natural area in Wisconsin, Parfrey's Glen is a site to behold. Situated within the boundaries of Devil's Lake State Park, this state natural area boasts some incredible natural features. A glen is considered to be a long, narrow valley accented by gently sloping sides, which tends to contradict what is at the end of Parfrey's Glen Trail: a deep, 100-foot ravine consisting of sandstone walls spotted with pebbles and boulders of quartzite. Because the glen is home to dozens of rare plants and insects (including some diving beetles!), it is of the utmost importance to stay on the trail.

Nearest town: Moon Valley

Getting there: For visitors entering the state natural area from the north/west on I-90, take exit 92 to merge onto US 12 east. Stay on US 12 for 7.3 miles and take exit 219. After a half mile, take a right onto Route 136 and continue on this road for 2.8 miles. Take a right onto County Road DL and continue for 2.6 miles, then turn right onto Route 113 south/County Road DL. After 2.3 miles, take another left to stay on County Road DL. You will see the entrance to Parfrey's Glen State Natural Area on your left. Park at the main lot on the right.

Trailhead: Parfrey's Glen Trailhead

GPS: N43 24.594' / W89 38.202'

Fees and permits: Wisconsin State Park Pass ($13 per day for residents, $16 for nonresidents)

Trail users: Hikers, trail runners (absolutely NO rock climbing)

Elevation gain: 209 feet

Length: 1.8 miles (out-and-back)

Approximate hiking time: Half day

Difficulty: Easy

Seasonal highlights: Due to its rocky ravine, the glen is prone to flash flooding and may close during nasty weather. Be sure to check the forecast prior to your trip.

Managing agency: Wisconsin Department of Natural Resources–Parfrey's Glen State Natural Area

Soaking in the views of Parfrey's Glen with Armani on her back DINEO DOWD

EXPERIENCING IT

Today, you're likely to find Dineo Dowd on the trail with her daughter at any given moment, exploring the nooks and crannies of a new route or bedding down in a tent for the night. The fresh air gives her inspiration and she strongly believes that nature is a confidence booster for her and Armani. However, she didn't always feel this way.

Born and raised in South Africa, Dineo grew up with a very different perspective of what hiking and camping adventures entailed. While she always had a keen interest in the outdoors, it never seemed readily available to her. As she explains it, her family did not have a lot of money so they would enjoy picnic adventures but could never swing more than that. Hiking involved additional gear so it was considered a luxury when staples like adequate food were tough enough to secure. Additionally, her region was fraught with crime, so much so that Dineo felt herself living constantly on high alert. A car following her on the highway was cause for concern in her world, so she never felt safe enough to stop at a trailhead or to explore a new hiking path by herself. Most people hired guides for hikes—a privilege Dineo couldn't afford—and hiking solo as a female was considered to be wildly unsafe.

Ultimately, Dineo grew up in an area where skin color dictated quite a bit of opportunity. Even when her family encountered hikers and campers at their favorite

The fall color in Parfrey's Glen is stunning! DINEO DOWD

picnic locations, everyone would just shrug off the activity as an impossibility. "Oh, we don't do that," her family told her. "That's just for white people." Thousands of tourists flood into South Africa annually, most hoping to enjoy a rugged safari or an outdoor wildlife adventure at any one of the world-class wilderness parks. But again, for Dineo and her community, these experiences weren't considered an option. "Why would we do that?" her friends would exclaim. "Are we trying to get ourselves killed?!"

Finally, after working fifteen hours a day and constantly wondering what else there could be for her out there, Dineo opted to take a break and move to the United States in 2012. As luck would have it, this break was a permanent relocation.

She first settled in Salt Lake City, Utah, where she immediately began exploring the outdoor scene. She discovered Hike It Baby and joined the group to help find camaraderie on the trail. After leaving South Africa, Dineo quickly realized how

Parfrey's Glen makes for a great child-friendly hike (Armani approved). DINEO DOWD

accessible hiking would be in her new life in the United States. Trails were plentiful; safety concerns were practically nonexistent; and her new friends at Hike It Baby helped educate her on the basic necessary gear. These exploratory hikes gave her the confidence she needed to keep going, to keep learning, and to keep pushing her newly acquired boundaries in the outdoors. Over time, she grew so self-assured in her abilities that she didn't fret when no one else showed up for the group hikes. Instead, she foisted her new baby into the kid carrier, packed the appropriate gear, and hit the trail by herself. It hadn't taken long before her self-doubt and worries from South Africa disappeared in her rearview mirror.

By the time her family relocated to Wisconsin, Armani was nearly two years old and had grown up on the trails. Dineo loved watching her daughter toddle down the soft dirt path, deeply squatting toward the earth in an effort to move closer to small insects and flowers that caught her short attention span. Armani didn't know any different; these trails were her home regardless of whether she lived in Salt Lake City or Madison. Watching her, Dineo realized it was time to do what she had done twice before: use hiking as a means to explore her new environment.

Dineo scoured the Hike it Baby hike offerings and found a nearby event for the upcoming week. The route was a new-to-her trail that sounded perfect for toddler legs: Parfrey's Glen. On the morning of the meet-up, Dineo remembers feeling like a bundle of nerves while driving to the trailhead. In Utah, Armani had thrived during these hikes, bouncing around between friends and smiling with glee whenever she spotted a snake or a strange-looking bug. But Wisconsin was a foreign place and neither Dineo nor Armani knew anyone. Would everyone be as friendly as in Utah? Would families even show for the hike? Gripping the steering wheel, Dineo worried that no one would come, leaving Armani heartbroken and searching for new friends.

WHAT IS PARFREY'S GLEN?

Most people don't think of cascading waterfalls, lush greenery, and towering canyon walls speckled with sparkling quartzite when they think of Wisconsin, but that's exactly what can be found at Parfrey's Glen. Parfrey's Glen is the Badger State's first state natural area, sandwiched inside Devil's Lake State Park, and it's become Instagram-famous thanks to its colorful and ethereal landscape.

In essence, the glen is a 100-foot-deep gorge cut into sandstone and filled with moisture from the swiftly moving Parfrey's Glen Creek. The walls are embedded with pebbles and quartzite, a conglomerate known as "plum pudding" stone that gives the canyon a bumpy sparkly effect. Thanks to the cool, shady environment, the glen feels like a real-life grotto with flora typically found in northern Wisconsin: yellow birch, red elder, and the state-threatened stemmed false foxglove, a pink, bell-shaped flower that blooms from late June to early September. The glen itself was formed by powerful water and that trend has continued over the past 20 years. Various thunderstorms ripped through the area in 2008 and 2010, destroying the boardwalks originally placed in the final section of the hike as well as the steps near the viewing area. As a result, the state stopped spending money on constantly repairing the trail and today's visitors will find a rustic approach that involves stepping through water and rough stone.

But all the concern was for naught. As the duo pulled into the parking lot, Dineo saw a group of mothers and children standing in the corner, waiting for the rest of the party to join. Armani spotted the crowd too and could barely wait for her mother to unclip the car seat and lift her out of the vehicle before eagerly toddling toward the group of future friends. A wide smile spread across her face as she smashed into the kids, enthusiastically hugging them as if she had known each one for years. It didn't matter to Armani that she had never met a single person in the bunch. For her, hiking meant friends. By that logic, these children were her dearest companions.

In watching her daughter busily float from kid to kid, Dineo realized how much she could learn from her 2-year-old. Armani was unphased by all of life's recent changes, and instead focused on the variables she was already familiar with: hiking and people. Her joy and excitement completely overshadowed any lingering concerns and Dineo saw that Armani was not afraid. Armani was going to go everywhere, as long as she was outside. And Dineo would join her.

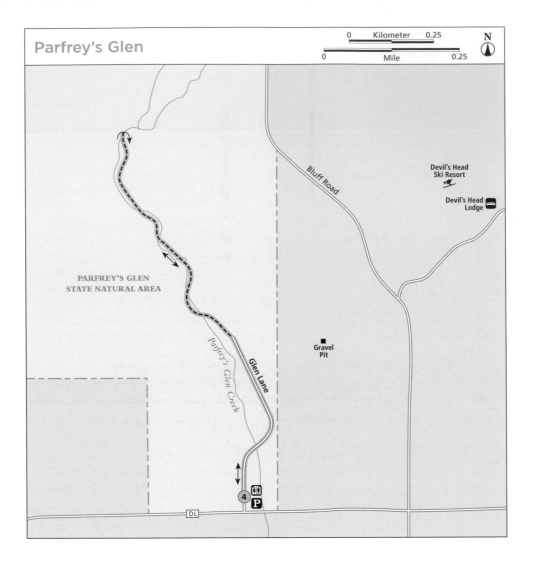

Parfrey's Glen

PARFREY'S GLEN
STATE NATURAL AREA

Bluff Road

Devil's Head
Ski Resort

Devil's Head
Lodge

Gravel
Pit

Parfrey's Glen Creek

Glen Lane

DL

THE HIKE

Begin hiking at the main parking lot for Parfrey's Glen State Natural Area. The trail starts off as a natural dirt path among wild raspberry bushes and then drastically turns into a deep ravine with moss-covered sandstone walls reaching upwards of 100 feet. The trail is short and fun for all ages. The start of the ravine marks the end of the maintained trail (due to many 100-year floods that hit the area, the Department of Natural Resources stopped maintaining the viewpoints along the trail). Visitors are allowed to go up to the small waterfall at the end of the ravine but are restricted from going any farther. Please adhere to all guidelines set forth by the Wisconsin Department of

Dineo in her happy place Dineo Dowd

Natural Resources to keep this area free of erosion and damage to a sensitive ecosystem. Return the way you came in.

MILES AND DIRECTIONS

0.0 Begin hiking at the Parfrey's Glen State Natural Area's main parking lot.

0.7 The end of the official maintained trail and start of the ravine.

0.9 Reach the end of the ravine and a small waterfall. Retrace your steps.

1.8 Arrive back at the trailhead.

CHERINE GIBBONS

Wedgemount Lake
Whistler, British Columbia, Canada

If you quickly glance at Cherine Gibbons's and her husband Roberto's exceedingly popular Instagram account, you're likely to assume that far-flung wilderness adventures have always been the norm for this mother of two. But you'd be mistaken. Born and raised in Senegal, Cherine (or Bella) moved to Montreal for university when

Cherine (Bella) with her husband, Roberto, and her children, Mikio and Catalina
ROBERTO GIBBONS

she was 18. She spent 4 years as a francophone studying biochemistry at an English-speaking school. Upon graduation, she met Roberto, who first introduced her to all things outdoors, including her first-ever camping trip with swarms of mosquitoes, a canoe—and two accidental black eyes.

Nearly 13 years later, the multilingual couple (Cherine speaks English, French, Arabic, and Wolof and Roberto speaks Spanish, French, and English) is married with two kiddos: Mikio (3) and Catalina (1). While their home base is in Whistler, Canada, the family jet-sets around the globe as content creators through various brand partnerships. When not traveling internationally, they're likely living off the grid in Happy, their Airstream trailer.

The drive from Vancouver to Whistler along the Sea-to-Sky Highway is like no other. As the highway curves and hugs the glacial cliffs and sea coast, you're never quite sure if you should be looking at the small specks climbing Squamish's Chief Mountain or the fins of orcas travelling through Howe Sound. Wedgemount Lake is found just north of Whistler, and although a short hike, it sits almost 4,000 feet above the start of the trailhead. Your legs may not be thanking you by the end of the day! This trail can be done as a long day hike (even though it's only 6.4 miles, the elevation gain proves for slow progress) or as an overnight where several campsites can be reserved, including a small hut. Be sure to spend some time (no matter the season) in the village of Whistler on your way out.

Nearest town: Whistler

Getting there: From Whistler, take the Sea-to-Sky Highway 99 north for 18.5 miles (11.6 km). Turn right onto Gravel Pit Road and then take a quick left at the fork. At the next fork, turn right on Wedge Creek Forest Service Road. Arrive at the trailhead, where the road ends at the parking lot.

Trailhead: Wedgemount Lake Trailhead

GPS: N48 17.622' / W124 39.906'

Fees and permits: No day-use fees, but a permit is required for overnight camping ($26.30 in Canadian dollars per night). Reservations must be made during the summer months due to limited spaces.

Trail users: Hikers, trail runners, backpackers, skiers, ice climbers, rock climbers

Elevation gain: 3,937 feet

Length: 6.4 miles (out-and-back)

Approximate hiking time: Full day

Difficulty: Strenuous

Seasonal highlights: Even on the hottest of summer days, the area surrounding this high-alpine lake can have quite a bit of snow, so look out for those summer ski bums.

Bella shouldering both kiddos on the way to Wedgemount Lake ROBERTO GIBBONS

Also come prepared in the summer months for lots of bugs! In the winter, the surrounding areas are popular for ice climbing.

Managing agency: British Columbia Parks–Garibaldi Provincial Park

EXPERIENCING IT

A mere half mile into the arduous uphill climb, Bella Gibbons came to an abrupt stop on the trail. With blood coursing through her veins and her heartbeat thumping louder than the surrounding chirping birds, she felt a familiar uneasiness rising from deep within her belly. "Oh God, Roberto, I think I'm going to puke!" she exclaimed to her husband. Her stomach lurched as her legs shook, completely taxed from the ungodly amount of human weight she was carting on her shoulders. In the past, Bella had hiked into many of the world's most remote backcountry locations, but this time was different. This time, she was carrying her two children—and their weight was annihilating her.

Hiking to Wedgemount Lake was nothing new for Bella. As Whistler locals, she and Roberto frequently tackled the near-perpendicular slog in an effort to create beautiful

---

TIPS FOR HIKING STEEP TERRAIN

With more than 3,900 feet of elevation gain in just over 3.2 miles, the hike to Wedgemount Lake is anything but easy. This trail is as vertical as they come! Here are a few tips to help you tackle the steeps.

- *Take small, slow steps.* Often called the "rest step," this technique is popular with mountaineers. Basically, move slowly and pause with every step, leaving your body weight on your back leg so the front leg is resting for a pause. Then, switch it up on the next step.
- *Take plenty of breaks.* Regular short breaks are always preferred to infrequent, longer rests.
- *Find your pace.* In a perfect world, you'll end the hike moving at a pace similar to the one used in the beginning. It may feel slow at first, but stick to it. Remember: The tortoise always wins the race!
- *Understand switchbacks.* Most established trails will switchback, or zigzag, up the hillside, and for good reason. This decreases the grade of the slope, which makes the gain feel more reasonable. If you're hiking off-trail, consider doing the same.
- *Stay positive.* Above all else, keep a smile on your face. Portions of the hike may feel uncomfortable, but remember: It's temporary. And the scenery at the end will always help you forget the discomfort along the way.

Stormy weather makes for great scenery as Mikio explores the lake. ROBERTO GIBBONS

content for their brand partners. The destination—a pristine turquoise lake sur-rounded by a rugged cirque of rocky ridgelines and peaks—was the ultimate backdrop for outdoor photographs. The wife-and-husband duo visited often. But during those previous adventures, one aspect was very different: Bella's pack weight. On previous trips, she was only carrying her gear and supplies, amounting to maybe 30 pounds on her back. Once, Bella and Roberto even carried Mikio to the lake for a few nights with Roberto carrying the gear and Bella carrying their son.

However, the Gibbons were now a family of four with the arrival of little Catalina. With the new addition came an added bonus: exponentially heavier backpacks.

Of course, Bella didn't have to hike to Wedgemount Lake. She and her family could have chosen any other (easier) backpacking trip in the area and likely enjoyed it just as much. But, as she is the first to acknowledge, it felt personal. Bella wanted to suc-cessfully climb to the lake to prove to herself that she could do it: She could still be the hardcore outdoor woman that she knew from the past decade. She just needed to try.

Bella soothes a tired Mikio as the sun glistens off the water. Roberto Gibbons

And so it went. While Roberto shouldered a monstrous pack, carrying the bulk of equipment for the foursome, Bella focused on their children. First, she loaded her 21-pound daughter into a soft front-carry system that allowed Catalina to nurse while Bella hiked. Then, she helped the 35-pound Mikio into a kid carrier before strapping him onto her back. Once both the children were comfortably seated atop their mother, Bella took a deep breath and placed one foot in front of the other.

But after a short half-mile distance, she collapsed on a rock in exhaustion. The weight of Mikio and Catalina sat heavy on her shoulders and her mind simply could not withstand the mental burden of knowledge: They still had 3,500 feet to climb with all of the difficult terrain ahead. Discouraged, she looked Roberto in the eyes and told him: "I'm giving up. I can't do this."

Yet she didn't get off the rock.

For the next 15 minutes, Bella considered all of her options. For a while, she wanted to turn around and head back to the trailhead so the family could find an easier, shorter hike. But even while her words conveyed a strong desire to leave, she never stood up. Gradually, she recalibrated and concocted a Plan B.

First, the couple dropped excess weight. They ditched Mikio and Catalina's sleeping bags, figuring the two children could share with their parents. Bella cut out the extra food, water, diapers, and layers. She stashed the surplus goods underneath a tree and then stood back to reevaluate the circumstances. Then, the duo worked out an

Camping on platforms is a welcome respite from the rocky terrain. ROBERTO GIBBONS

alternating system. First, Bella would carry both children. Then, Roberto would take Catalina and carry her with his backpack, giving Bella a needed reprieve while she carried only Mikio. They continued this way—slowly but surely—up the mountain.

Higher and higher she climbed with her two babies in tow. Catalina kept herself busy breastfeeding, constantly reminding Bella of her presence by consistently yanking at her nipple. Mikio sat in the kid carrier, relatively bored with the scenery and playfully leaning from side to side, oblivious that the shifting of his weight flung his mother around the trail. Yet Bella continued.

But time was not on their side. Bella's slower pace combined with the late start meant the family was racing sunset. As the sun dropped lower and lower on the horizon, she felt the evening temperatures chill as they often do in the Canadian high country. Mentally frazzled but still determined, she told herself to move faster. "If you hike quicker, we can still make it to the lake tonight," she thought.

Eventually darkness fell. At 9:30 in the evening, Mikio began sobbing in a clear signal to his mother: The kids were done for the day. Still ascending the precipitous hillside, the family couldn't see a single flat location to pitch a tent. Frustrated, Bella too began to cry, weary from the day's efforts. "I did my part, Roberto," she sobbed. "I got the kids up here. You figure it out and build them a tent."

It wasn't the best, but Roberto created a home for the night by securing the tent to a few trees that prevented the nylon shelter from sliding downhill. Bella, Mikio, and Catalina immediately crawled inside while Roberto slept outside in the dirt. It wasn't how Bella imagined their first night at Wedgemount Lake, but she didn't have much time to ponder their situation before she drifted off to sleep.

Morning came late for Bella and her babies as they slept off the previous day's exhaustive trials. For Roberto, however, the sunrise began early. He awoke in the predawn hours and loaded up his backpack before hiking the remaining 2 miles of loose talus up to Wedgemount Lake. Once there, he dropped his pack and jogged back down the mountain to his waiting family. There, he took Mikio from Bella so she only had to carry Catalina through the remaining difficult sections of trail. Then, as a family, the foursome continued upwards until they arrived at Wedgemount Lake.

They pitched their tents on the same rocky ledge that Bella and Roberto had previously camped on, knowing the prime location had the best views of the lake. And for four days and nights, the little Gibbons family basked in the sunshine and splashed in the brisk glacial waters of Wedgemount. The trip had not been what Bella expected, but she likes to say that she learned more about her family through such a tiring experience.

"I know my limits, but I realized my limits changed with the kids," she explains. "There is always a solution. Talk it over with your partner and find that solution and you'll find those new limits."

THE HIKE

Begin your hike at the gravel parking lot at the Wedgemount Lake Trailhead. There is minimal incline at the beginning stages, which gives you a false sense of what this trail really has in store for you. After crossing the creek by taking two sets of bridges, you'll start the steep incline (and the countless switchbacks) through several rock slides in the area. This is also why this trail is extremely difficult in the winter time and should only be hiked by those with avalanche safety training. The final section of trail up to the lake is the steepest and is extremely rocky and slippery, especially during wet conditions (which, in British Columbia, is most of the time). Take note of the weather and make sure everything is clear before heading up to the lake. Once there, enjoy a well-deserved break and snack before the grueling descent back to your car.

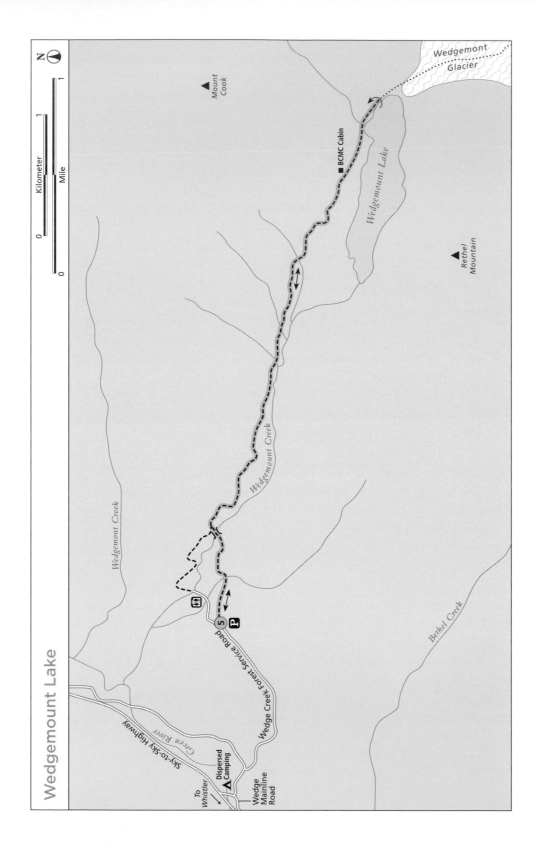

Wedgemount Lake

MILES AND DIRECTIONS

0.0 Wedgemount Lake Trailhead.

0.5 Cross two bridges over Wedgemount Creek.

1.2 Come to a rock slide and follow the trail markers up into the trees.

2.1 Final rock slide, where the vegetation starts to thin and the ascent steepens.

2.8 Wedgemount Lake and the British Columbia Mountaineering Club cabin come into view.

3.2 End at the northern side of Wedgemount Lake. Begin the steep descent back.

6.4 Arrive back at the trailhead.

6

ILANA JESSE

Pikes Peak via the Barr Trail
Colorado Springs, Colorado

Ilana Jesse, 37, is an emergency department trauma nurse at one of the busiest Level 1 trauma centers in the state of Colorado. While she initially received a chemistry degree from the University of California, Los Angeles (UCLA) with the intention of going

Ilana Jesse ILANA JESSE

to medical school, she later opted against that career path for fear that it would take her away from her patients. As a result, she spent 5 years in medical small business development. But she felt completely unfulfilled in that industry so she went back to healthcare and nabbed a nursing degree.

In addition to her work as a trauma nurse, Ilana is also a sponsored trail runner for Dynafit, a European-based outdoor brand with strong footholds in alpine sports. Ilana helps the brand with gear development ideas and Dynafit supports her long-distance running efforts, like her 2019 and 2020 attempts at Nolan's 14. The aptly named unofficial run is a roughly 100-mile route that climbs up and over the 14 "fourteeners" in Colorado's Sawatch Range, logging a massive 42,000 feet of gain while doing so.

Ilana is married and lives in Colorado Springs with her husband and daughter, Amari, age three.

Towering over the city of Colorado Springs at 14,115 feet above sea level, Pikes Peak can be enjoyed via hiking, driving, or even by train car. Although you can drive up this fourteener (there are only two peaks in the United States that make this possible!), there is nothing compared to the joy of walking up with your own two feet. Starting in the lovely artistic town of Manitou Springs, the Barr Trail starts just farther down the road from the Pike's Peak Cog Railway. It's a long and grueling climb with the last mile being the hardest, and the journey requires a lot of mental strength. If you have the stamina to make it to the top, you'll be well-rewarded with views and world-famous donuts to replenish all those lost calories.

Nearest town: Manitou Springs

Getting there: Take I-25 to exit 141 for US 24 West. Stay on US 24 for 5.5 miles and then take a left toward Manitou Springs (opposite the road for Cave of the Winds). At the traffic circle, take the second exit onto Manitou Avenue. At the next traffic circle, take the first exit onto Ruxton Avenue. Just after the Pike's Peak Cog Railway, turn right onto Hydro Street and park in the small parking lot.

Trailhead: Barr Trailhead

GPS: N38 51.342' / W104 56.040'

Fees and permits: $10 per day parking fee

Trail users: Hikers, trail runners, backpackers

Elevation gain: 7,401 feet

Length: 24 miles (out-and-back)

Approximate hiking time: Full day (if you get a ride down from the top) or overnight at Barr Camp

Difficulty: Strenuous

Seasonal highlights: This trail should only be attempted by seasoned hikers and during good weather. Typical summer thunderstorms arrive in the afternoon, so be prepared.

Managing agency: US Forest Service–Pike National Forest

Ilana and her daughter begin the journey up Pikes Peak. Ilana Jesse

EXPERIENCING IT

2018 was one hell of a year for Ilana Jesse.

While Ilana is now known for her athletic ultrarunning pursuits on the high peaks of Colorado, that wasn't always the case. In fact, just a few years ago, she identified as an alpine climber, a branch of climbing that involves long approaches and multiple pitches of roped climbing on high alpine peaks. She spent most of her time rock and ice climbing, including the first female ascent in 2015 on a 5.12+ rock-climbing route called "Shock Treatment" in Colorado. But that all changed on May 12, 2018.

The following morning was her first Mother's Day with her new daughter, Amari, but instead of lounging with breakfast in bed all day, Ilana was camped out on a glacier in Alaska with a few climber friends. Their original goal was to summit Mount Hayes (13,832 feet), the highest peak in the eastern Alaska range. But, due to bad weather, the climbers shifted their focus to Mount Skarland, a modest 10,315-foot peak to the northwest of Hayes. It should've been a relatively easy expedition for this team, but Mother Nature had other plans.

While scrambling up the peak, a freak rockfall incident sent a wave of boulders crashing down the hillside. Ilana looked up just in time to see one of the larger rocks bouncing toward her. She vaguely remembers hearing her friend yell, but the distressed cries faded into blackness as Ilana lost consciousness. She awoke a few minutes later to realize that the errant boulder had smashed her left hand, leaving her with a

---

WHAT IS A FOURTEENER?

If visiting Colorado, you're likely to hear a local throw out the term *fourteener* (or *14er*). It's a phrase as common as *hello* in the Centennial State, but for those visiting from sea level, it may sound like gibberish. What in the world is a fourteener?!

A fourteener is a peak over 14,000 feet in elevation. In the entire United States, there are 96 fourteeners, all of which sit west of the Mississippi River. In fact, the bulk of these peaks live in Colorado; the state alone has 58 while Alaska is a distant second with 29 (although Alaska's peaks take the top 22 spots with Mt. Denali measuring up at a whopping 20,310 feet). The tallest fourteener in the lower 48 states is Mt. Whitney in California at 14,505 feet, but Colorado's Mt. Elbert is a close second at 14,440 feet. Pikes Peak, the mountain referenced in this chapter, is number 30 in Colorado at 14,110 feet. If you don't feel like hiking, Pikes is one of two fourteeners in Colorado with a road to the summit (Mt. Evans is the other). Thanks to the Manitou and Pikes Peak Railway Company, Pikes Peak also boasts the highest cog railway in North America, offering visitors a variety of options to get to the summit.

Ilana during one of her many training runs on the Barr Trail ILANA JESSE

mangled raw mess of crushed bones and bloody tendons—and they were still miles into the backcountry.

Thankfully, Ilana remained conscious and her medical background helped her friends stop the blood loss and stabilize her long enough to evacuate her more than 1,200 feet down the mountain. From there, the team was able to activate the SOS feature on their personal locator beacon to call for help. A waiting helicopter found Ilana on the Hayes Glacier and whisked her away to the nearest hospital, where the doctors did everything they could to salvage her hand and avoid amputation.

One year later, Ilana was still grappling with the effects of that day on Mount Skarland. More than ten surgeries saved her hand but left her with what she calls a "panda thumb," or a nonopposable thumb. She lost complete feeling and can only handle eight pounds of pressure, but she can still hold a can of food and has adapted to her life as a trauma nurse. However, she could no longer climb. Her identity as a climber was gone.

"To this day, people refer to me as an alpinist and that's not really who I am anymore," Ilana says. "But I struggled for a while because I had to figure out who the new me actually was."

To battle these demons, she headed to the mountains, where she had always found solace. She couldn't use her hand, but her legs still worked so she began hiking. As time passed, she hiked farther and farther. Then, she started moving faster and faster. Before she even realized it, she morphed into a strong and able ultrarunner.

Simultaneously, Ilana was learning to adapt to her new normal as a mother. She'd heard the age-old adage too many times to count: *Hardcore athlete becomes a mom and settles down in life*. And honestly, reality would've made that an

Turns out, Colorado's fourteeners are a veritable playground for toddlers! Ilana Jesse

easy choice and certainly one that most would understand thanks to her recent climbing accident. But Ilana didn't want that. She wanted to be a role model for Amari, exemplifying a powerful woman who didn't allow life's obstacles to get in her way.

So she kept running and she kept hiking. Often, she would hike with her husband and Amari, loading the toddler up in the kid carrier and carrying her up the hillside. These trail respites took her away from the constant surgeries and mangled memories tearing up her brain. While hiking, Ilana could focus on her family and their goodness rather than process the complicated changes happening back in the real world. It was after one of her last surgeries that she and her husband decided to take Amari up Pikes Peak.

Fresh off the operating table, Ilana was still wearing a sling so it was questionable for her to be hiking the 24-mile round-trip route up and down the fourteener looming outside of Colorado Springs. But her physical therapist also understood that Ilana

Ilana and Amari keep hiking above the tree line. ILANA JESSE

wasn't like most other patients. When Ilana requested her blessing, the therapist simply shrugged and said, "Okay, but if it gets too tender, put the sling back on. Please bring the sling!"

Her husband carried Amari since Ilana could not, and the trio began their hike on what was becoming one of Ilana's favorite training areas. It was a big day post-op, but Ilana focused more on the time with her family. Amari was finally old enough to understand the alpine environment around her, so Ilana took the opportunity to explain the pikas and the marmots scampering around the landscape. Amari climbed on the rocks above the tree line and the family celebrated when the toddler successfully used the bite valve on the hydration pack for the first time (rather than a sippy cup). It was an amusing benchmark when compared to her mother's previous feats in the Alaskan high alpine, but it was the perfect cherry on top of an already wonderful day.

Beyond the sippy cup evolution, the family's hike on Pikes Peak was a personal transition for Ilana, too. After accomplishing such a long day with a bum hand, Ilana knew she was ready for the next phase. She had faith that she could learn to trust herself again in the mountains and set her sights on a challenge that suited the next chapter: Nolan's 14. No, it wasn't climbing and it probably wouldn't ever be again. But she'd discovered a new means to push herself and test her mettle. She'd found another way to become a better human—and a better mom.

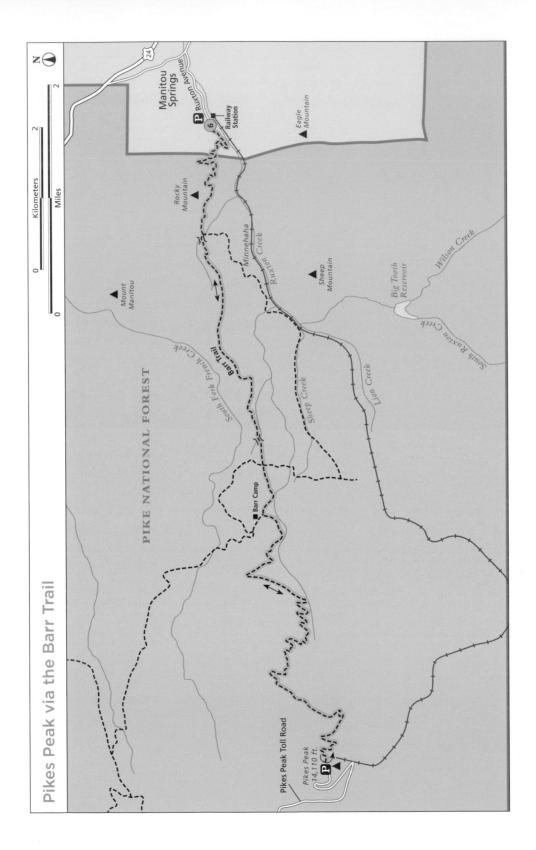

Pikes Peak via the Barr Trail

N

Kilometers
0   2

Miles
0   2

PIKE NATIONAL FOREST

Manitou Springs

24

Ruxton Avenue

Railway Station

Eagle Mountain

Rocky Mountain

Minnehaha

Ruxton Creek

Mount Manitou

South Fork French Creek

Barr Trail

Barr Camp

Sheep Mountain

Sheep Creek

Lion Creek

Big Tooth Reservoir

Wilson Creek

South Ruxton Creek

Pikes Peak Toll Road

Pikes Peak
14,110 ft.

THE HIKE

The trail begins steeply and you'll gain almost 4,000 feet in elevation in the first 6 miles. The first 3 miles of that will be mostly steep, tight switchbacks that seem never ending. Make sure to stop at Barr Camp whether you are staying overnight or for a much-needed rest. From there, the 2 miles after the camp are gentle and ease back into the climb ahead. As the trail starts to ascend more steeply, you'll find an A-frame style hut here where you can rest or stay (it's unmanned and used on a first-come, first-serve basis). At the "three miles to the summit" sign, make sure to take the narrow trail where the hardest part of the climb begins. The air gets quite thin and your breathing will become shallower. Make sure to take deep breaths and watch for signs of altitude sickness. Make the final push to the summit where you can enjoy those famous donuts at the Summit House. Many hikers have a ride ready for the way down, but if you're a true diehard, make the trek back down to your car the same way you came up. (And give yourself a pat on the back!)

MILES AND DIRECTIONS

0.0 Begin hiking at the Barr Trailhead near the hydro plant.

0.6 The start of the steep switchbacks.

3.0 The trail becomes much gentler and gives your legs a much-needed reprieve.

5.9 Barr Camp where you can stop and eat or stay overnight.

6.8 Stay left to continue on Barr Trail.

9.0 "Three miles to the summit" sign and the start of the hardest part of the trail. Make sure you have the stamina to continue the hike.

12.0 Arrive at the Summit House and enjoy the view. When you're ready, hop in your prearranged car ride down or hike the 12 miles back to your car.

24.0 Arrive back at the trailhead.

CAITLIN LANDESBERG

The Ninja Loop
San Francisco, California

Caitlin Landesberg, 37, is the founder and CEO of Sufferfest Beer Company, a brand focused on low calories, high standards, and gluten-removed beers. Brought to market in 2016, Sufferfest came as a result of Caitlin's lifelong affinity for two things: running and beer. As a former competitive tennis player in Ohio, she found running once she moved to California for a job with Strava. Running and Strava fit together as smoothly

Caitlin Landesberg MICHAEL McSHERRY

as peanut butter and jelly, and Caitlin quickly grew into an avid ultrarunner, hitting the trails as frequently as possible. But in 2011, Caitlin was diagnosed with Hashimoto's disease, a chronic condition in which the immune system attacks the thyroid. Among other solutions, doctors suggested Caitlin eliminate gluten from her diet— including her beloved finish-line beers. In an effort to find a solution, Caitlin began home brewing gluten-free beverages. Over time it took off, and within 3 months of her launch, Sufferfest Beer was found in every Whole Foods in the Bay Area. The widescale growth continued for this athlete-specific beer, culminating in the 2019 first-ever acquisition by beer giant Sierra Nevada Brewing Company.

Caitlin is married with two children (ages 2 and 4). Still an avid runner, she is a member of Brooks Off-Road Running, an ambassador team of trail runners for shoe brand Brooks Running.

The Ninja Loop is known fairly well by local outdoor enthusiasts. It is usually a trail run but can be a long day hike as well. Because of its location within the Golden Gate National Recreation Area, its trails can be swarmed by tourists enjoying the views of the Golden Gate Bridge. However, if hiked early in the morning, this strenuous trail will not only feel secluded but will also encourage those avid trail runners aching for their next ultramarathon. After all, there is nothing more motivating than sweeping views of the iconic Golden Gate Bridge as well as the surrounding Pacific Ocean.

Nearest town: San Francisco

Getting there: From San Francisco, take US 101 north to exit 442 and follow signs for the North Tower Golden Gate parking lot.

Trailhead: Golden Gate Bridge parking lot

GPS: N37 49.950' / W122 28.920'

Fees and permits: Parking fees are enforced 10 a.m. to 5 p.m. daily ($1.20 per hour or $7 per day).

Trail users: Trail runners, hikers

Elevation gain: 2,614 feet

Length: 11.9 miles (loop)

Approximate hiking time: Full day hiking, few hours trail running

Caitlin running in the hills outside of her home in California MICHAEL MCSHERRY

Difficulty: Strenuous

Seasonal highlights: Beautiful views of the Golden Gate Bridge, San Francisco, and the surrounding ocean exist year-round, but there is little shade on the entirety of the trail. Be prepared for heat in the peak of summer and cold winds in the winter.

Managing agency: National Park Service–Golden Gate National Recreation Area

EXPERIENCING IT

Caitlin Landesberg was only 3 months postpartum when she realized how dramatically life had changed.

One Friday evening, one of her girlfriends called her up with an interesting proposal. "Let's run Ninja this weekend!" she requested, her voice filled with excitement. "It'll be great. You're back!"

Caitlin hung up the phone feeling a mixture of emotions. For the most part, her competitive drive reared up from deep inside her, practically taunting her to tap into those

WHAT'S SO SPECIAL ABOUT GOLDEN GATE NATIONAL RECREATION AREA?

It is easy to look at Golden Gate as just another urban park, but this extensive and diverse national recreation area (NRA) is arguably one of the most complex parks in the United States. For starters, it protects more than 82,000 acres of land, ranging from historical landmarks to ecologically significant sites. That is more than twice the size of San Francisco itself! Unlike other NRAs in the country, Golden Gate is spread out between southern San Mateo County and northern Marin County via a collection of sites. Some of the most notable include Alcatraz, Muir Woods National Monument, and the Presidio of San Francisco.

Beyond its historical importance, Golden Gate also boasts a unique array of terrestrial, marine, and coastal environments. The United Nations Educational, Scientific, and Cultural Organization (UNESCO) designated the entire park a UNESCO Biosphere Reserve and the International Coalition of Sites of Conscience dubbed Golden Gate an International Site of Conscience. This is all largely thanks to the forty-four species of butterflies, a diverse bird population, and the twelve designated rare, threatened, or endangered plants all found within the park's boundaries. And finally, hikers and walkers alike love this part: Dogs are allowed! Golden Gate is the only park in the National Park Service to designate special areas for responsible off-leash dog walking.

primal feelings. After years as a competitive tennis player and then runner followed by a successful career as a female business owner, Caitlin knew a thing or two about inner drive. Even the word *ninja* incited a frenzy in her brain, reminding her of all those predawn runs before her daughter was born. During the early morning hours while the world still slept, she and her friends would meet at the trailhead near the Golden Gate Bridge Vista Point, shining headlamps bouncing on their foreheads. Together, they'd tackle the punishing terrain as it undulated throughout the 12-mile loop, harshly climbing from sea level to 1,000 feet in just 1 mile. Then, Ninja plummeted back down again like a rollercoaster only

The unassuming start to the Ninja Loop
CAITLIN LANDESBERG

to repeat the vicious hilly cycle a few more times. The runs were always grueling and relentless yet Caitlin kept coming back again and again.

But she had yet to revisit the Ninja Loop since Fran was born. While her core group of friends was just starting families of their own, Caitlin was one of the first to actually birth a babe. She admired her friends' enthusiasm, but there was a small part of her that wondered whether she was ready for Ninja. Still, she quelled the nerves and gave herself the pep talk she needed to tackle the following day.

Motherhood isn't going to hold me back. It's time to return to all of the things I love. I can do this, no problem. I'm feeling strong. I'm ready to go.

These words ran on repeat in her mind as she prepared for Ninja that evening and woke up the next morning. But just as she managed to assuage her cognitive dissonance while stumbling around her darkened house in the twilight hours, her brain pumped the brakes faster than traffic at a red light.

"Oh my god, what about my breast pump?!"

In her sleepy stupor, Caitlin thankfully remembered her body's maternal needs. Since she would be running for a few hours and away from her daughter, she needed to concoct a plan to empty the milk from her breasts. Haphazardly, she threw her breast pump in the car while tying her shoelaces and searching for her car keys. Before starting the engine, she hooked the pump up to herself so that she could begin extracting the milk while she drove to meet her friends. Caitlin knew they would be ready to go once she arrived and she didn't want herself—or her motherhood—to be the reason anyone experienced a late start. She didn't want to mention it to her friends either. Caitlin wanted today's Ninja Loop to be just like all the older ones. So instead, she made a mental note for next time:

I'll just get up 30 minutes earlier so I can handle this at home.

Still, she wasn't yet done with pumping by the time she reached the trailhead. While her girlfriends sat in the car next to her eating their traditional pre-run bananas, Caitlin hid in the darkness of her own vehicle, listening to the whiny mechanical sounds of the pump as it sucked in and out. Finally, frustrated with all of the time she was wasting for everyone, Caitlin shut off the pump and declared herself ready. It was time to run.

The first few steps on the trail felt like a homecoming. Her lungs welcomed the intake of oxygen as she deeply inhaled the sweet salty air wafting in from the Pacific Ocean. Her feet found a rhythm, gracefully kissing the soft earth with every single step. She felt good and the morning's chaos subsided from memory as she ran alongside her friends.

But after a few minutes, she realized they were done warming up. As the trio's pace quickened, her feet cycled faster and faster in an effort to keep up with her athletic companions. Her breath grew ragged and she felt a thunderous pounding in her

The flat terrain near the beginning makes for a great warmup for the hills to come.
CAITLIN LANDESBERG

tailbone, while her hands began to visibly tremble. Still, she didn't want to slow the group down so she persevered, lagging farther and farther behind. By the time the runners reach the Bobcat Trail climb—the toughest section of the loop—her pelvic floor felt weaker than a tissue. She tried the same self-talk that had worked the previous evening, reminding herself of how she used to scamper up the impossibly steep climb. But on this day, in this new body, it was all for naught. Bobcat may well have been a wall for all her body cared. She was done.

Caitlin slowed her pace to a walk, trudging uphill through a thick ocean fog darker than the clouds in her mind. She watched as her friends disappeared into the mist, seemingly full of energy and life. Meanwhile, her breasts ached and her body swelled as she slogged her way through the remainder of Ninja. She even took a wrong turn since the old loop was as foreign to her as her new life. She stumbled back to the trailhead, weaving and lost in sheer embarrassment as her friends clapped her back to the car in celebration. But she didn't want to be clapped back; that wasn't her. And this wasn't anything to celebrate.

Family, running, and beer: three things that make Caitlin smile Caitlin Landesberg

She wallowed in her discomfort at the trailhead and during her drive home. She quickly dubbed that morning "Lost in a Fog" because that was how she felt: lost. After her performance, Caitlin realized that life was not going to be the same after motherhood. After all, she wasn't the same. Somewhere along the way, she felt a relentless pressure to be just like pre-baby Caitlin, but that wasn't possible. Something had to give, and she finally realized that only she could decide what new Caitlin actually enjoyed in this strange alternative reality. For some runners, that may be returning to where they were prior to childbirth, but that wasn't Caitlin. Over time, she accepted that constantly comparing her running performance and behavior with her old self was frustrating at best and completely demoralizing at its worst. Ultimately, it brought her pain and sadness at what she lost. Caitlin wanted to focus on the life she was building—not the one that would never return.

A few years later, Sufferfest partnered with REI on a 10K run. As luck would have it, the chosen course was the Ninja Loop. Even more fortuitously, Caitlin was once again 3 months postpartum with her second daughter. Her entire team peppered her

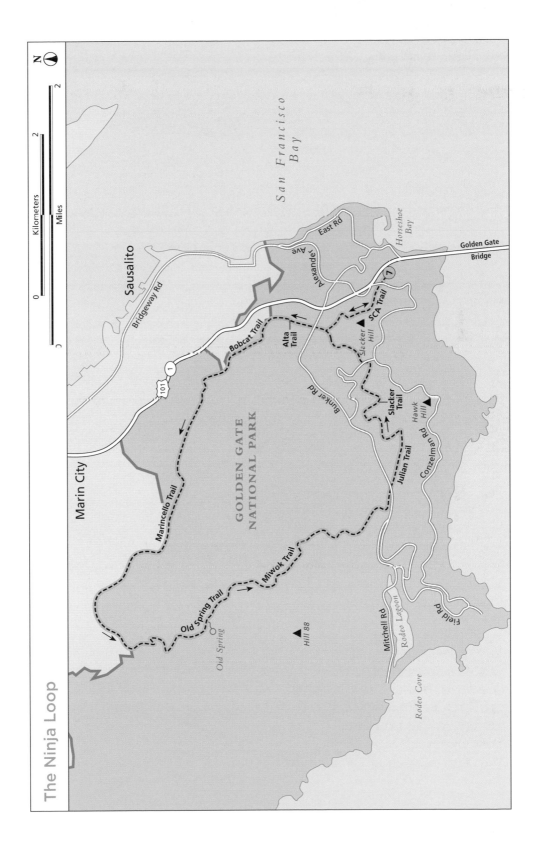

The Ninja Loop

with questions of encouragement: "Are you going to run it?" "Are you going to win it?" But Caitlin opted to acknowledge where she was at in her new life, with this new body, and her newfound self-confidence that allowed her to make decisions without shame or regret. Instead, she watched runners come into the finish line while playing with her daughters. She didn't run and she certainly didn't win.

But she did have fun.

THE HIKE

Make sure to start this hike early before the crowds of tourists arrive so you can secure your parking spot (and seclusion on the trail). Begin your hike at the North Tower parking lot in the Golden Gate National Recreation Area just north of the bridge. Start out on the Coastal Trail—the first of many trails that make up this 12-mile loop. It climbs steadily up toward Slacker's Ridge and onwards along the SCA Trail. Running along Miwok and Marincello Trails, you are rewarded with incredible views of the ocean and surrounding attractions including the iconic Golden Gate Bridge. Make sure to stop and take in the sea breeze coming off the cliff edge before heading down the valley and back to your car.

MILES AND DIRECTIONS

0.0 Begin the trail run at the Coastal Trailhead from the North Tower parking lot.

0.3 Meet up with the SCA Trail.

1.2 Continue on the SCA Trail (fork right).

1.4 Keep left to stay on the SCA Trail.

2.0 Pick up Alta Trail.

2.6 Take a left onto Bobcat Trail.

3.0 Take the right fork to stay on Bobcat Trail.

3.3 Continue onto Marincello Trail.

4.9 Follow signs to Miwok Livery Stables and continue onto Old Spring Trail.

6.1 Take a right onto Miwok Trail.

6.4 Take the left fork to continue on the Miwok Trail (do not take Wolf Ridge Trail).

7.5 Take a left onto Rodeo Valley Trail.

7.9 Take a right onto Julian Trail.

9.6 Take a left onto Slacker Trail.

10.7 Take a right back onto SCA Trail.

11.6 Take the Coastal Trail.

11.9 Arrive back at the trailhead.

AMELIA MAYER
Phelps Lake Loop Trail
Jackson, Wyoming

Amelia Mayer is a 38-year-old mother of five children (ages 11, 9, 6, 4, and 2) and the founder of *Tales of a Mountain Mama*, an online website dedicated to stories, tips, and product reviews that educate and inspire families to get outside. Born and raised in Palmer, Alaska, Amelia strongly disliked playing outside until she found Nordic ski racing in high school. From there, outdoor recreation followed her into college and then married life.

Thanks to her husband's job with the National Park Service, Amelia and her family actually live within the boundaries of Great Teton National Park, where they can explore world-class terrain directly from their backyard. Through *Tales of a Mountain Mama*, Amelia is able to turn her daily adventures with her kiddos into user-friendly information and resources for her growing audience. But, above all else, she hopes to inspire other families by showing that outdoor families are just like everyone else, and that it is possible.

Amelia Mayer AMELIA MAYER

There are many reasons to take a trip up to Laurance S. Rockefeller Preserve within Grand Teton National Park, including the parking lot cap of 300 visitors per day (compared to around 5,500 for other parts of the national park). So, if seclusion is what you seek within a very popular national park, look no further. Within the 1,106-acre preserve, there are more than 16 miles of trails, including ones that are ADA accessible and used as interpretive trails. Whether you are a differently abled individual, a poet searching for their next muse, or a family of seven needing a break from each other, the Phelps Lake Loop Trail is for you.

Nearest town: Jackson

Getting there: For visitors entering the preserve from the south on US 191, take a left on Teton Park Road toward Moose. Follow this road for 0.7 miles and then turn left on Moose-Wilson Road. After 3.7 miles, turn left into the Laurance S. Rockefeller Preserve and park.

Trailhead: Lake Creek Trailhead

GPS: N43 37.596' / W110 46.398'

Fees and permits: Day users need an America the Beautiful Interagency Pass ($80 per year) or a Grand Teton National Park day pass ($35 per vehicle).

Trail users: Hikers, trail runners

Elevation gain: 475 feet

Length: 7.2 miles (loop)

Approximate hiking time: Full day

Difficulty: Moderate

Seasonal highlights: The road into Laurance S. Rockefeller Preserve is closed seasonally from November to May but you can still ski, snowshoe, or hike in during those months.

Managing agency: Administered by Rockefeller Foundation and National Park Service–Grand Teton National Park

EXPERIENCING IT

Societal norms often view motherhood as one of life's greatest highlights—and it is. But so often, these glittering perspectives on a woman's entrance into motherhood

Meet the entire Mayer family AMELIA MAYER

discount the sadness and loneliness that new moms frequently experience. In fact, if a mama isn't medically diagnosed with postpartum depression, her despondency is often overlooked. In reality, nearly 80 percent of mothers experience the *baby blues*, a sudden change in hormones that causes new mamas to feel anxious, sad, or lonely.

Amelia Mayer was one of these women. In fact, she experienced the baby blues on repeat: five times for her five children.

The flat portions along Phelps Lake are perfect for little legs. AMELIA MAYER

After her eldest was born, Amelia struggled to regain normalcy in her life. It was physically harder to get out the door and mentally demanding to even consider the possibility. Dishes stacked up and laundry piles grew, contributing to the looming feelings of anxiety that niggled at the dark corners of her already consumed mind.

Then, she and her husband welcomed their second child into the world. Then their third. Each time, the baby blues poked their way into her conscience, a persistent reminder that life's great joys are not met without equally complicated pushback. And even though she had been down this road before, the blues never grew easier or more manageable. Instead, she simply learned how to persevere through them, wading through the mental cobwebs until a glimmer of sunshine appeared on the other side.

For Amelia, that usually happened while hiking. Once she put foot to trail, the overcast emotions lifted from her shoulders, granting her a brief respite from life's woes. As long as she was outside with her family, her sanity returned.

By the time she and her husband had their fourth child, she felt a bit more prepared. But still, after her daughter joined the family, Amelia felt the familiar tug of despondency. This time though, her situation exacerbated those intimate feelings of loneliness as she tried to find her identity as a mom. Thanks to her husband's career, the family had recently relocated to Jackson, Wyoming, for one of his work details. It was a dream come true and they were ecstatic to be living in such a pristine wilderness area with ample outdoor opportunities. But with only a few months of Jackson living under their belts, Amelia felt unrooted.

Then she experienced one of life's greatest tragedies: the loss of a loved one. A dear friend passed away exactly one week after childbirth, leaving her baby behind and Amelia's heart in pieces. There she was, nursing her own fourth child while also helping to nurse her friend's newborn at the same time. The sorrow was suffocating and Amelia struggled to cope with the simultaneous loss of her friend and the recalibration of her new world with another child. As she wrestled with the heavy emotions threatening to overwhelm her, she made a decision: She would not go through this again. No more children.

Of course, the world rarely listens to our plans. Less than 6 months later, Amelia and her husband received the delightful news: They were expecting their fifth child. While overjoyed with love for their impending addition to the family, Amelia immediately

TIPS FOR HIKING WITH MULTIPLE CHILDREN

It's one thing to hit the trail with a baby in tow, but how do you handle it with two children? Three children? Or, how in the world will it work with five children of varying ages?! Fortunately, Amelia is a pro at hiking with all five of her kids in tow, so she offered up some of her best tips.

- *Choose trails with a variety of terrain.* In doing so, older children have plenty to keep them entertained while the younger kids can enjoy bonus snack or rest breaks.
- *Toughen up.* If you want to hike at a big-kid pace, you will likely need to carry the younger children yourself. Amelia recommends the occasional bribe in the form of music or special hiking-only snacks. Or, consider a trade: The parent carries the young children on the way up but they can stretch their little legs on the return downhill.
- *It takes a village.* If you have children of varying ages, consider inviting along another family. Not only will the kiddos positively encourage each other, but the adults can tag team with the remaining children to accommodate various speeds.
- *Peer guidance.* Amelia suggests allowing the older children to help and encourage the younger kids. By using this buddy system, everyone has a job while encouraging the pack to stay together.

The lake itself provides endless fun. AMELIA MAYER

felt a wave of conflict wash over her. Not only was she still struggling with the tragic loss of her friend, but her body had not yet recovered from her fourth child. With her fourth and fifth kiddos arriving a mere 18 months apart, Amelia felt wildly off kilter and unprepared for such an impactful sequence of events.

She felt emotionally exhausted and mentally destroyed. So she did the only thing that had ever helped her survive in the past: She hiked.

While her husband was away fighting fires, Amelia challenged herself to get outside with her children every single day. Some days, it went really well. Others were less successful with more than 2 hours of organized chaos before they headed out the door. But with each subsequent attempt, Amelia felt lighter. Every morning, she'd line up the snacks and gear needed for a day hike with her four children. Her two eldest boys were old enough and strong enough to hike on their own, so she often tasked them with helping her prepare her two smaller kids.

Amelia's sons lead the way through the early fall color.
Amelia Mayer

There were a number of trails they visited, but Amelia often found herself heading back to a local favorite: the Phelps Lake Loop Trail.

Often, it was as if a circus rolled into town when the five of them hit the dirt. The boys would run ahead, hooting and hollering as they stretched their legs alongside their vocal chords. Inevitably, one of her daughters would scream about staying home or wail over a belly ache (that miraculously disappeared 5 minutes into the hike). Amelia would bring up the rear, carrying her youngest babe in a kid carrier on her back while protecting her soon-to-be-fifth child in her belly. They never moved quickly or efficiently and the Mayer's trail progress looked significantly different than her hikes a decade ago. But Amelia felt grateful.

Pregnancy still terrified her. She still carried a void left by the loss of her friend. And baby blues still tiptoed around in the shadows. But while all of these emotions swirled together in a melancholy melting pot, she felt something else: strength.

The last six months had been difficult, but here she was. Amelia was still hiking down the trail, watching her children scamper along the horizon while carrying another two

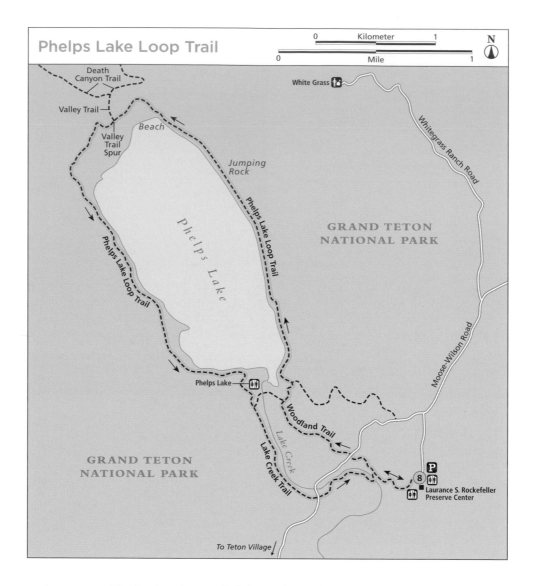

Phelps Lake Loop Trail

on her person. Her husband was still fighting fires. The sun was still shining. The water was still glistening.

Despite everything that happens, life goes on. And it will continue to do so.

In that moment, the trail gave her the connectedness she needed to move forward. It gave her the strength. It gave her the courage. Her body could—and would—do this again.

THE HIKE

Begin your hike at the parking lot at Laurance S. Rockefeller Preserve and head toward the visitor center. Feel free to pop into this platinum LEED-certified building and learn about its history. There are two ways to go around Phelps Lake but going counterclockwise is the more scenic route, so stick to the Woodland Trail. The trail circles this 750-acre lake (the sixth largest in Grand Teton National Park), home to osprey searching for their next prey. As you meander through the evergreen forest, the lake provides enough viewpoints of Death Canyon and the surrounding mountains. If you're feeling gutsy, take a walk over to Jumping Rock (a not-so-secret boulder perfect for jumping into the lake) and take a dive into the water. If sitting and relaxing is more your style, then head farther down the trail to Phelps Beach to lay out a towel and sunbathe. On the latter half of the hike, make sure to cause a ruckus going through the huckleberry patches as bear frequent this area during the spring and summer months. Head back to your car by linking back up with the Lake Creek Trail.

MILES AND DIRECTIONS

0.0 Begin hiking at the Lake Creek Trailhead, heading towards the Laurance S. Rockefeller Visitor Center.

0.3 Reach a trail junction. Stay right at the fork to follow Woodland Trail.

1.3 Take a right onto Phelps Lake Loop Trail.

2.5 Reach Jumping Rock.

3.1 Lounge at Phelps Beach—you earned it!

4.0 Keep left at the fork to continue on Phelps Lake Loop Trail.

5.3 Reach a three-way junction and take the middle trail for Lake Creek Trail.

6.2 Cross the Aspen Ridge Trail and continue on Lake Creek Trail.

6.9 Reach the first trail junction and follow signs back to the parking lot.

7.2 Arrive back at the Lake Creek Trailhead.

9

CHRISTINA MCEVOY
Havasu Falls
Supai, Arizona

Christina McEvoy CHRISTINA MCEVOY

Christina McEvoy, 42, is the voice behind Macs-Explore.com and the accompanying popular Instagram account. Christina, her husband, Eric, and their two sons, Carson (12) and Austin (15), left behind their routine life in early 2019 in favor of slowly traveling the world. They first headed to Central America where they spent 8 months exploring everywhere from Guatemala to Colombia. Then the family caught a flight to South America where they lived for an unplanned five months in Chile during the novel coronavirus quarantine before heading north to Ecuador. Christina says the quartet will return to the United States in 2021 so Carson and Austin can enjoy "normal" teenage school activities, but she is a strong advocate for educational travel and experiences.

While abroad, Eric works as an online physical therapist and Christina manages her online course, Insta-Success. This step-by-step program walks students through the process needed to turn their Instagram accounts into successful and profitable travel brands. Christina is also a loud voice in the outdoor community, encouraging parents with teenagers to spend time outside. While she acknowledges that the outdoors can't cure everything, she does believe that more time in the sunshine could be a great healer for societal issues affecting teens such as depression and low self-esteem.

Increasing in popularity since these turquoise waters graced social media, Havasu Falls is much more breathtaking in person than on a phone screen. Due to its famous and unreal color, the hike to Havasu Falls is only obtained via an online permit. It sells out almost immediately so you'll have to be ready the minute permits go on sale. Even then, it isn't guaranteed that you'll snag one (as Christina discovered!). If you're lucky enough to get permission to walk these hallowed grounds, it'll be an adventure you won't forget. The beauty of these waterfalls is only found after a grueling 10-mile hike along the red rock canyon, a stark and joyous contrast to the aquamarine waters that await you at the end.

Nearest town: Flagstaff

Getting there: For visitors entering Havasupai Tribal Reservation from the east on I-40, take exit 121 toward Route 66. Follow Route 66 for almost 30 miles, then turn right onto Indian Road 18 and continue for 60 miles, where the road ends and where you'll park for your journey at the Hualapai Hilltop parking lot.

Trailhead: Havasupai Trailhead

GPS: N36 09.576' / W112 42.564'

Fees and permits: Backpackers need a permit obtained online beginning on February 1, 8:00 a.m. Arizona time ($100–$125 per night per person) each year. All permits are for a 3-night excursion, no exceptions.

Trail users: Backpackers

Elevation gain: 2,346 feet

Length: 20 miles (out-and-back)

Approximate hiking time: Multi-day backpack

Difficulty: Strenuous

Seasonal highlights: Due to its southern desert location, the best time to visit is shoulder season when temperatures are more manageable (April–June and September–October). July through August is monsoon season, which has historically caused backpacker evacuations due to flash floods.

Managing agency: Havasupai Tribal Nation

EXPERIENCING IT

When Christina and Eric were married in 2000, they made a promise to each other: They would live an adventurous life. Their family motto—*We Can Do Hard Things*—perfectly aligned, challenging the couple to continue pushing themselves outdoors, whether it be through cultural immersion or heart-pounding wilderness exploits. So when the duo first heard about Havasu Falls in 2003, they were immediately intrigued.

At that point, the travertine-filled water was lesser known since social media had yet to popularize the cascading falls deep within the Grand Canyon. But permits were still required and Christina and Eric applied with little success. Havasu Falls would have to wait.

Time passed and their family grew. Christina birthed Austin first and then Carson. As the family learned to navigate life as a quartet, Havasu Falls was relegated to the back burner, although they continued to explore their home state of Idaho. But in 2010, Christina was dealt a massive setback when she was diagnosed with stage 4 melanoma, an aggressive form of cancer that began with a mole on her thigh but subsequently spread to a lymph node near her groin and then into multiple tumors in her lungs. Stage 4 melanoma is often difficult—if not impossible—to cure, but Christina jumped into her

The McEvoy Family CHRISTINA McEVOY

The hot and dry hike in (and out!) of the canyon can feel interminable. CHRISTINA MCEVOY

treatment with the same fervor she uses in every aspect of her life. She flew back and forth from Boise to San Francisco to meet with her doctor, and often combined holistic treatments with the more mainstream Western medicine. In her words, she threw everything "including the kitchen sink" at her illness because she was going to live.

And she did. 2020 marked her tenth year in remission, a survival rate that the American Cancer Society says only 10–15 percent of patients hit. But as the years clicked through to 2015 and 2016 and Christina reached her earlier 5-year-remission goal,

The travertine-filled
waters of Havasu Falls
are an impossible shade
of blue. WILL ROCHFORT

WHO ARE THE HAVASUPAI PEOPLE?

Havasu Falls sits tucked away along Havasu Creek in the Grand Canyon, outside of national park boundaries but very much inside the Havasupai Native American Reservation. The Havasupai people (People of the Blue-Green Water) have lived in the Grand Canyon for more than 800 years. While they are one of six tribes still affiliated with the region, they are the only people to still reside deep within the canyon walls today.

Originally, the Havasupai were nomads who farmed, hunted, and gathered at the base of the canyon, using the pristine blue waters as a means of irrigation and sustenance. However, settlers began moving west in the late 1800s and many found their way to Havasu Falls to stake mining claims. Tensions increased over the beautiful land. As a result, in 1882 President Hayes relocated most Havasupai onto a 518-acre parcel, minimizing access to their own territory. The forced removal continued in 1919 when the Grand Canyon National Park was established, further infringing upon Indigenous lands. But the Havasupai continued to fight for what was theirs. Thanks to a series of legal battles, the government returned 185,000 acres to the Havasupai people beginning in 1975. Today, there are more than 600 tribal members, many of whom still live in the canyon. While they can no longer subsist on a hunter-gatherer lifestyle as they once did, the Havasupai continue to honor and respect their ancestor's traditions. To fill in the gaps, they have taken over the tourism component for Havasu Falls, employing many of the locals in the cafe, lodge, tourist offices, or via guiding. All of the proceeds from Havasu Falls go directly to the tribe, helping them flourish into the twenty-first century.

she began mentally revisiting unfinished dreams from before her world was flipped upside down. Once again, she returned to Havasu Falls.

Her sons' spring break vacation was creeping up so Christina decided that the whole family could head to Havasu Falls, finally allowing her the chance to visit the aqua pools she had first learned about more than a decade ago. But in 2016, her permit application was denied. She applied again in 2017 and, for the third time in her life, was once more denied. But she didn't give up. In 2018, Christina applied for Havasu Falls permits once more—and they were accepted.

After spending nearly $600 on permits (the prices have since risen) to visit the impossibly idyllic oasis in the Grand Canyon, Christina and her family were determined to do it up. She crafted an itinerary that gave them 3 days in the canyon and nearly 35 miles of hiking after it was all said and done. It would be the highest mileage Carson and Austin had ever tackled in such a short window of time, but Christina

felt confident in their abilities. And she wasn't wrong. The McEvoy family thrived at Havasu Falls, laughing as they splashed in the jewel-toned water, and voyaged down toward Mooney Falls. They stayed up talking beneath the glittering sky before flopping into their hammocks where they passed out from the day's physical exploits. Havasu was everything that Christina had dreamed it would be all those years ago.

But it was also tiring. By the time the third day rolled around, everyone was exhausted, especially 10-year-old Carson. As the family packed up their heavy backpacks to begin the 10-mile hike out with nearly 2,500 feet of elevation gain, Carson looked at his mother with pleading eyes. "Mom, could we hire a donkey to carry our backpacks out?" he asked.

Christina understood her son but also wanted him to realize this hike out of the canyon would strengthen him physically and mentally. She told him no. "You carried your pack into the canyon; you can carry it back out," she told him. "We'll take lots of breaks along the way. You can do this. *We can do hard things.*"

They toiled upwards, doling out brief snack breaks with Carson's favorite candy, Sour Patch Kids, as bribery. Every 15 or 20 minutes, Christina gave Carson a couple of the gummy treats to encourage forward progress amidst the litany of complaints. *I can't do this. This is too hard.* And to be fair, the terrain was difficult. As the McEvoy family neared the top of the canyon rim, the terrain hit peak steepness, climbing roughly 1,000 feet in the last mile. Carson struggled upwards, eventually giving his

Aside from Havasu Falls itself, a number of cascading waterfalls line the canyon. WILL ROCHFORT

Trekking through the water feels wonderfully refreshing on a hot spring day. Christina McEvoy

backpack to his father to carry. He was running on fumes and the last mile felt like the past 34 combined. Still, he kept hiking while his mother encouraged him with affirmative platitudes and sweet-and-sour candies.

Finally, they made it: Christina and her family stood atop the canyon rim with all 35 miles of hiking in their rearview mirror. In celebration, the foursome promptly ripped the backpacks from their shoulders and collapsed to the ground. Their bellies heaved with exertion as they laid in the dirt, sweat running down their faces and pooling in the dry Arizona heat. Eventually, Christina and Carson mustered enough energy to sit upright and soak in the memories of the past few days.

After enough time passed, Christina turned toward her son and asked: "How do you feel?"

"Mom, I'm really tired," Carson responded with a deep sigh.

"No, I know that, but how do you feel? Are you glad you did it?" Christina pressed.

She watched her youngest son as a mishmash of emotions plainly rolled across his face. He clearly wanted to craft an appropriate response and she grew nervous. "*What if I was wrong and he absolutely hated it?*" she wondered to herself.

After a few minutes of silence, Carson finally gave her an answer. "I didn't see any other kids my age hiking."

"Yeah, most of them were Austin's age or even adults," Christina agreed.

"I just barely turned 10," Carson continued. "So that's pretty cool that I hiked 35 miles with a pack by myself and you guys didn't have to help me, you know?"

Christina smiled as she watched Carson piece it together. Often, parents feel like they need to spell the lessons out for their children in the hopes they glean the good stuff. But as she watched him, Carson was doing it all by himself. *We can do hard things.*

THE HIKE

Start your journey at the Havasupai Trailhead and promptly descend down to the canyon floor. Begin your hike early to avoid the hottest parts of the day as there is no shade within the canyon walls. You'll get through most of the descent within the first 2 miles, and from then on, it's a fairly flat walk to the falls. It's a relatively easy trail to navigate since it's so popular, but stay alert to make sure you stick to the trail. Along the way to the falls, make sure to stop by Supai Village to confirm your reservation and pick up your wristband that you'll have to wear for the remainder of your trip. Before making it to Havasu Falls, you'll be greeted by two other ones: Fifty Foot Falls and Navajo Falls. Since you have to make a three-night reservation, definitely continue to Mooney and Beaver Falls after you reach Havasu and the campground. The trail can be sketchy after Havasu Falls so enter at your own risk. After you have absorbed as much of the teal-blue waters as humanly possible, retrace your footsteps out of the canyon and back to your car. Give yourself plenty of time since it's all uphill on the way back and will likely take you longer.

MILES AND DIRECTIONS

0.0 Begin hiking at the Havasupai Trailhead.

1.7 Reach the canyon floor, where the trail will level out.

4.1 Canyon starts to narrow. Be wary of flash floods.

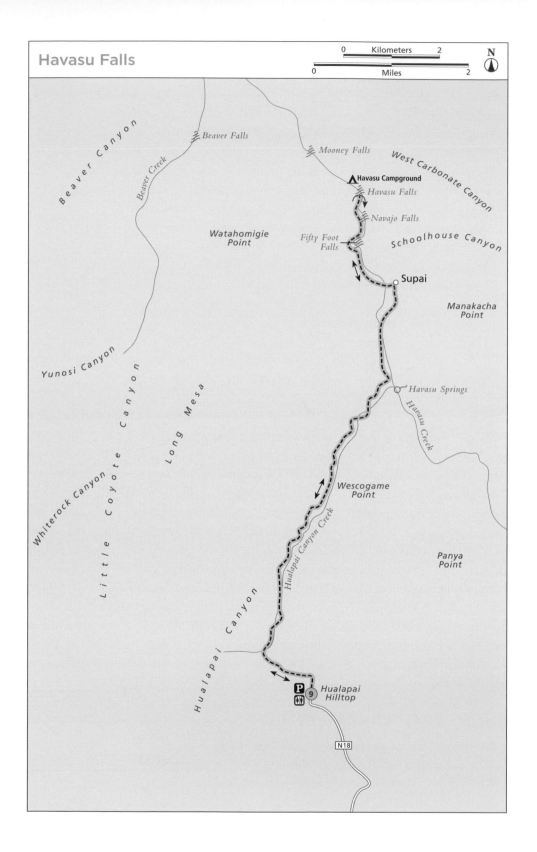

Havasu Falls

0 — Kilometers — 2
0 — Miles — 2

N

Beaver Canyon

Beaver Falls

Beaver Creek

Mooney Falls

West Carbonate Canyon

Havasu Campground

Havasu Falls

Watahomigie Point

Navajo Falls

Fifty Foot Falls

Schoolhouse Canyon

Supai

Manakacha Point

Yunosi Canyon

Havasu Springs

Havasu Creek

Whiterock Canyon

Little Coyote Canyon

Long Mesa

Wescogame Point

Hualapai Canyon Creek

Panya Point

Hualapai Canyon

P
9
Hualapai Hilltop

N18

7.9 Reach Supai Village and register at the tourist office.

9.1 Reach Fifty Foot and Navajo Falls.

10.0 Reach Havasu Falls. Enjoy your few days on the Havasupai Tribal Reservation* and then retrace your steps back to the trailhead.

20.0 Arrive back at the trailhead.

For additional hikes during your journey, Mooney Falls is 0.5 mile and Beaver Falls is 3.5 miles past the campground.

10

NATALIYA MOON

Jade Lake
Cle Elum, Washington

Nataliya (Natasha) Moon, 35, is a Ukrainian content creator and children's book author who uses her platform to show that outdoor adventure is still possible with children. Born and raised in Kharkiv, Ukraine, Natasha grew up in a concrete jungle, living on the eighth and thirteenth floors of a massive apartment building in the second-largest city in the country. Aside from her summers spent in the nearby villages, Natasha didn't

Nataliya Moon and her daughter, Zoey JACOB MOON

have much exposure to hiking until she immigrated to Italy when she was 18. There, she learned all about hiking and skiing and snowboarding and camping and her interest was piqued. By the time she came to the United States for school at the LDS Business School in Utah, Natasha was very interested in the outdoors.

Today, Natasha and her husband make their living as content creators via their two wildly popular Instagram accounts where they have amassed more than 210,000 followers. Last year, they lived out of their renovated Sprinter van while traveling the country, finding and sharing imagery and stories from beautiful wilderness places as they went. Their daughter Zoey, age 3, joined in on the fun and frequently appears in Natasha's stories about outdoor adventure. Moreover, Natasha released her first self-published children's book in 2020. Entitled *Adventure to the Top of the Mountain*, the story chronicles a brave little girl named Zoey who wants to hike to the top of a nearby peak.

In recent years Jade Lake has become extremely popular, and for good reason. Set in the heart of Mt. Baker–Snoqualmie National Forest, Jade Lake attracts photographers, nature lovers, and wildlife enthusiasts with its majestic azure waters from the Lynch Glacier. Jade Lake is usually enjoyed on an overnight trip but can be seen during a long, adventurous day hike if you have the gumption. You'll be rewarded with an abundance of wildflowers, lakes that are "out-of-this-world" in color, and mountain goats aplenty. But make sure to bring your best bug spray as the mosquitos are harsh and plentiful here as well.

Nearest town: Cle Elum

Getting there: For visitors entering Alpine Lakes Wilderness from the west on I-90, take exit 80 and turn left onto Bullfrog Road. After 2 miles, take the first exit in the traffic circle to stay on Bullfrog Road. At the second traffic circle, stay straight to head north onto Route 903. After a mile and a half, turn left onto West Nevada Avenue and then right again to stay on Route 903 North. Stay on Route 903 for 4.5 miles, when it turns into Salmon La Suc Road, and continue for another 10 miles. Continue onto FR 4330 for 12 miles. The road ends at the trailhead.

Trailhead: Tucquala Meadows Trailhead

GPS: N47 32.616' / W121 05.784'

Fees and permits: A National Forest Recreation Day Pass ($5 per day), Northwest Forest Pass ($30 per year), or America the Beautiful Interagency Pass ($80 per year) must be displayed on the dashboard of your vehicle. You must carry the self-serve

wilderness permit (free at the trailhead) if camping overnight.

Trail users: Hikers, trail runners, backpackers

Elevation gain: 4,284 feet

Length: 20.6 miles (out-and-back)

Approximate hiking time: Full day or overnight

Difficulty: Strenuous

Seasonal highlights: Summertime in this area brings out the best of wildflower displays and, with it, lots of mosquitos as well. Make sure to come prepared with a good camera for the flowers and bug spray for mosquitos. If you're hanging out at Jade Lake for a bit, keep an eye out for mountain goats.

Managing agency: US Forest Service–Alpine Lakes Wilderness

EXPERIENCING IT

Many new mothers go into their first pregnancy with high expectations and a clear outline of how they want childbirth to go. While some of those women are fortunate to experience their ideal birthing scenario, many others learn their first lesson in parenting: Nothing goes as planned. Natasha Moon was one of the latter. Heading into her pregnancy with Zoey, Natasha was confident in her birth wishes: no drugs, a midwife, and labor at home. In short, she wanted the natural experience she had always dreamed of when envisioning her daughter's entrance into this world.

The wonderfully blue waters of Jade Lake
Jacob Moon

WHY IS JADE LAKE SO BLUE?

It doesn't matter if you are a world traveler or if you haven't ever left your home state. Anyone who comes upon Washington State's Jade Lake for the first time has a similar reaction: *How in the world is this beautiful water so blue?!* At first glance, it is easy to see where the stained-glass pool earned its moniker. But at second glance, jade doesn't even begin to describe the ethereal milky blue-green color. As it turns out, Jade Lake's hue doesn't come from the heavens but instead from the powerful movement of a glacier.

It is known by a few names, with rock flour or glacial flour being the most popular. As the nearby Lynch Glacier moves down the hillside in something called glacial migration, the bottom of the glacier grinds against the rocks beneath it. This process, known as glacial erosion, is a persistent and robust grating that pulverizes the rocks into a very fine-grained, powder-like substance—just like sandpaper. This substance is rock flour. Then, as bits and pieces of the glacier melt, the rock flour is carried into the lake, completely suspended in the meltwater due to its miniscule size. This suspended rock flour is called glacial milk since it frequently causes the meltwater streams to take on a milky blue color. From there, the water flows into Jade Lake where the rock flour remains suspended. When the sun's rays hit the tiny particles, the water absorbs the long-wave colors like red and yellow and orange. The rock flour itself absorbs the short-wave colors like purple and indigo. Meanwhile, the remaining colors—mainly green and blue—reflect off the rock flour, so those are the only hues our eyes acknowledge.

But near the end of her second trimester, Natasha received some unwelcome news. She had noticed that her stomach was uncomfortably large, but she chalked that up to pregnancy in general. After all, the baby needed space to grow, right? Eventually, she and her husband met with a doctor who confirmed her concerns. The obstetrician diagnosed Natasha with a rare condition called polyhydramnios that occurs in approximately one out of one hundred pregnancies.

Polyhydramnios is when the mother has way too much amniotic fluid, the liquid that surrounds the baby inside the uterus. While this fluid does protect the babe from outside blows, too much of it can be incredibly uncomfortable for the mother since it increases the size of the womb, which then presses on the internal organs and lungs. Minimally, this causes breathing issues and stomach pain. But more severe potential symptoms include placental abruption, premature rupture of the membranes, premature birth, or even stillbirth.

Natasha and Zoey sleeping in the tent JACOB MOON

Natasha was devastated. Not only was the last trimester of her pregnancy wrought with stress and worry over her baby girl, but she also knew that her wish for a natural childbirth was gone. Due to the high-risk nature of her condition, her doctor advised that she labor in a hospital under medical supervision. In another lesson on parenting, Natasha birthed Zoey via an emergency C-section. It wasn't what she once imagined, but she no longer cared: She had her beautiful baby girl.

But the hits kept coming. In addition to the sleepless nights and routine lifestyle adjustments that inherently come with a baby, Natasha experienced low breast milk that found her and her family in the hospital one night with a severely dehydrated daughter. Formula entered the equation. And her severe postpartum back pain simply wouldn't go away. The shooting agony felt so crippling at times that she found herself unable to walk—a massive inconvenience with a new baby and certainly for a woman who once lived her life outside. After mentioning it a few times at checkups and not receiving any solutions, she began researching the symptoms herself. That's when Natasha realized the truth: She had diastasis recti, a partial or complete separation of the abdominal wall where your belly pokes through. While common in new mothers, it can be massively inconvenient and uncomfortable and doesn't always go away through postpartum physical therapy. And even though nearly two-thirds of mothers experience the muscle separation, health insurance typically considers it a cosmetic problem and won't cover treatment or the subsequent surgery since it is performed by a plastic surgeon.

Frustration didn't even begin to explain how Natasha felt. She tackled physical therapy and now says abdominal surgery may be in her future. But in the meantime, she needed to care for herself. Her emotions varied drastically, swinging from absolute

The ethereal waters of Jade Lake with Lynch Peak looming in the background JACOB MOON

devotion to her new baby girl to utter demoralization at the fact she couldn't even sit up from the ground without rolling onto her side first.

"I felt broken," she says. "I was totally defeated and felt like nature had betrayed me."

As she and her husband usually did before Zoey's birth, they found solace outside. The family began car camping since it was easy enough for Natasha's body. They eventually graduated to day hikes, starting with 30-minute adventures and working up from there. After nearly 12 weeks of Natasha burying her frustrations with daily trail time, the Moon family opted to head to Jade Lake for their first family backpacking trip.

Looking back, Natasha now remembers the trip as one of the hardest physical challenges she has ever endured. The 10.3-mile journey to Jade Lake climbed thousands of feet in elevation and nearly undid her. As she willed herself closer and closer to Jade's azure waters, she found herself trapped in a mental comparison game.

I used to roll up this hill.
It never felt this hard before.

But still, she continued moving, constantly reminding herself that she was no longer that person. She pushed herself, harder and harder, perhaps passively linking Jade Lake with her new self. If she made it to Jade, she'd make it.

Natasha made it to the lake, of course. She and her family spent three wonderful days exploring the glittering water while introducing Zoey to their favorite family pastime. But in yet another lesson on motherhood, Natasha had one more trial to overcome. The night before the family hiked back to the trailhead, she spiked a massive fever. Today, she is unsure what caused her to get so sick, but she has her suspicions. Her depleted physical state combined with her insatiable need to persevere may have weakened her body to an unsalvageable level. Regardless, the voyage back to the car felt interminable. Unable to maintain a straight line, Natasha weaved around the trail and frequently stumbled in her efforts to make forward progress. Her husband exclusively cared for Zoey because Natasha was simply unable to manage anything more than a single step at a time. But, as any outdoorswoman can attest to, there was nothing to be done. The only thing standing between Natasha and a needed respite was herself.

Playtime in the tent JACOB MOON

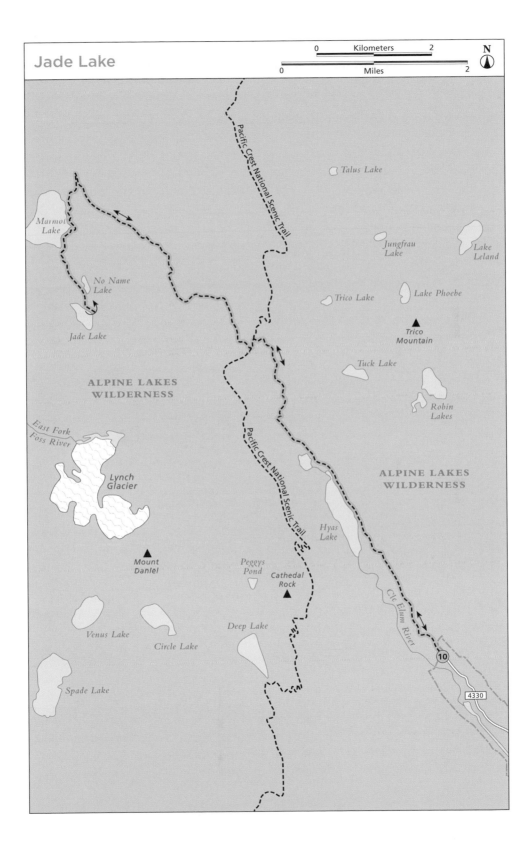

Jade Lake

0 Kilometers 2
0 Miles 2

N

Pacific Crest National Scenic Trail

Talus Lake

Jungfrau
Lake

Lake
Leland

Marmot
Lake

No Name
Lake

Trico Lake

Lake Phoebe

Jade Lake

Trico
Mountain

ALPINE LAKES
WILDERNESS

Tuck Lake

Robin
Lakes

East Fork
Foss River

Lynch
Glacier

Pacific Crest National Scenic Trail

ALPINE LAKES
WILDERNESS

Hyas
Lake

Mount
Daniel

Peggys
Pond

Cathedal
Rock

Cle Elum River

Venus Lake

Circle Lake

Deep Lake

10

Spade Lake

4330

So she continued, moving slower than she had ever hiked before. Each step lasted an eternity and her shallow breathing echoed in the hallways of her mind. *One step*, she told herself. *Just one step*. Bit by bit, Natasha worked her broken body back to the trailhead. And as she finally saw the glimmering reflection on her car's windshield, she burst into tears.

The tears were puddles of sadness as she accepted that her body was fallible; she couldn't handle anymore—or at least, not right now. But the streams rolling down her face also represented a deep and perverse joy in her accomplishment. That day—and the past few months—had felt impossibly hard, yet here she was, demonstrating that she could do hard things.

THE HIKE

Begin your hike at the Tucquala Meadows Trailhead, found at the end of the dirt road. The first few miles of the trail are fairly flat and easygoing. In no time, you'll reach Hyas Lake before beginning a steep incline up the valley. When you reach the top of the first stretch of switchbacks, you'll cross over the Pacific Crest Trail. Make sure to stay straight and continue onto Marmot Lake Trail. After ascending another series of steep switchbacks, you'll reach Marmot Lake, which is a mere 1.5 miles from Jade Lake. Stop for a quick break and snack and head the rest of the way to your destination. There are several camping spots along the trail but make sure to practice Leave No Trace principles and stay 200 feet away from paths and bodies of water.

MILES AND DIRECTIONS

0.0 Begin hiking at the Tucquala Meadows Trailhead at the end of the dirt road.

1.9 The trail skirts the eastern side of Hyas Lake.

3.5 Begin steeply ascending up the valley.

4.8 Cross over the Pacific Crest Trail.

6.6 Start the steady climb to Marmot Lake.

8.8 Reach Marmot Lake.

10.3 Reach Jade Lake. Retrace your steps back to the trailhead.

20.6 Arrive back at the trailhead.

11

CHELSEA MURPHY

Wedge Mountain
Leavenworth, Washington

Chelsea Murphy is a San Diego-born, Washington-raised social and environmental activist whose aim is to create a true "outdoors for all" world. Based in Leavenworth, Murphy is equally passionate about adventure and speaking about social injustices, so she uses her wildly popular Instagram account to simultaneously tackle both conversations. She firmly believes that environmentalism cannot exist without social equity and encourages her followers to engage in conversation in an effort to dismantle deeply embedded systemic racism, specifically in the outdoors.

However, as a married mother to her two daughters, ages 3 and 7, Chelsea is the first to say that her diversity work is not her top priority. Instead, the focus of her efforts ties back to raising her two children. She tries to spend at least 30 minutes outside every day with her girls, if only so they can see a strong Black woman on the trails and know that anything is possible.

Chelsea Murphy CHELSEA MURPHY

Most say the hardest part of this hike is not the scramble up to the summit; it's the treacherous road you take guiding your vehicle up to the parking area. If you manage to navigate your vehicle (a four-wheel-drive, high-clearance car is required) to the parking area, the quick rock scramble up to the summit offers spectacular views of the Enchantments without the need for one of those coveted permits. Known mostly to locals, this unnamed trail is not maintained by any agency, though the Washington Trails Association does acknowledge its existence. There is some debate about where the true summit of Wedge Mountain sits (and we won't get into that here), but this trail and the ridge along it bring you to breathtaking scenery and an unforgettable experience.

Nearest town: Leavenworth

Getting there: For visitors entering from the north on US 97, continue 4 miles south and turn west onto FR 7300 (Mountain Home Ranch Road). Follow FR 7300 to a right turn up a steep hill (signed "Mountain Home Road/Leavenworth") and continue 2.5 miles. Turn left onto FR 7305 and continue along a moderately rough and rutted road (there are a few other small dirt roads but follow the most-used track). At a fork at around 4,000 feet, go straight ahead and follow this to a large parking area at around 4,500 feet. The last section is narrow, rutty, and most definitely requires a high-clearance vehicle. It is best to check the road conditions prior to your adventure. If you find the route impassable, consider turning around and trying another day.

Trailhead: Unnamed trailhead

GPS: N47 29.934' / W120 41.376'

Fees and permits: Northwest Trail Park Pass ($5 per day) or an America the Beautiful Interagency Park Pass ($80 per year)

Trail users: Hikers, scramblers

Elevation gain: 1,706 feet

Length: 3.0 miles (out-and-back)

Approximate hiking time: Half day

Difficulty: Moderate

Seasonal highlights: Due to its remote location along dangerous and narrow logging roads, this trail should only be accessed during clear weather to ensure a passable road. High-clearance vehicles are required, not just recommended.

Managing agency: None (it is a social trail not maintained by the US Forest Service–Okanogan-Wenatchee National Forest)

EXPERIENCING IT

Wedge Mountain signified many firsts for Chelsea Murphy.

The 6,885-foot behemoth looms over the picturesque community of Leavenworth, practically beckoning hikers to play along the monstrous north–south ridgeline that constitutes its summit. With exceedingly steep slopes to the east and west, Wedge boasts magnificent views of the Alpine Lakes Wilderness and the Enchantments Lakes, making it a crowd favorite—for those who know it's actually hike-able.

For a period of time, Chelsea wasn't entirely sure she could make it to the top. While pouring wine at a restaurant in downtown Leavenworth, Chelsea often glanced up at Wedge's granite face, wondering at the possibilities. No matter where she went in town, Wedge was a backdrop that constantly reminded her of its presence. So she took to the internet, researching deep within Google to find information about the peak lording over her life. Not only did she find trail beta, but she also realized it was

---

WELCOME TO LEAVENWORTH

If you visit Leavenworth, Washington, today, you'll probably feel like you stepped straight into Bavaria. That's no accident, but you may be surprised to learn that Leavenworth doesn't actually have any German roots!

Prior to the 1900s, the land now referred to as Leavenworth was prime hunting ground for the Yakama, Wanatchee, and Chinook Indigenous tribes. Elk and deer were plentiful and Icicle Creek was teeming with salmon. However, by 1890, settlers moved into the area in search of gold and timber, creating what was originally known as Icicle Flats. The arrival of the train at the turn of the century sent the community reeling and set the logging and sawmill businesses booming. But of course, the timber industry was temporary. When the railway rerouted its path and left the area, the population of Icicle Flats plummeted so low that it could practically be considered a ghost town. The community fumbled along in silence for nearly three decades. But then, in the 1960s, the leadership concocted a brilliant marketing scheme. Everyone said the surrounding hillsides were just as beautiful as those found in Bavaria, so why not provide a German-like town in North America? Everyone got to work, completely renovating the downtown buildings and creating German-inspired festivals like the Autumn Leaf Festival and the Christmas Lighting Festival. The transformation was a success, bringing millions of tourists annually who want to experience "Bavarian authenticity with Northwestern hospitality."

Working her way up to the summit
CHELSEA MURPHY

possible: She could hike Wedge Mountain. Now she needed a plan, and she started with her mind.

Not only would Wedge be her first-ever hike over 10 miles (she needed to hike some of the approach road, too), but it would also be her most difficult adventure yet. With nearly 1,700 feet of elevation gain in the last 1.5 miles alone, Wedge's near-vertical route is not for the faint of heart. Up until this point, Chelsea's hiking resume included moderate trails with fewer obstacles and significantly less sweat equity. But Chelsea knew she was capable so she began recruiting company.

"This really was a 'third time is the charm' scenario!" she laughs.

The first time she headed up with a friend, they found the road washed out so far below the lower trailhead that they could not continue. The second time, she and another friend ran into a large moose who was none too happy about sharing the road with a lowly Subaru. But after that, Chelsea was determined to hike Wedge Mountain. She approached one friend who grew up in the area, certain that she would be interested in joining. She was surprised to learn that Wedge held an aura of mystery for the lifelong local, too.

Hiking through a sea of wildflowers CHELSEA MURPHY

"She asked me to help her get up there," Chelsea remembers. "She had tried so many times and failed so she had started to doubt it was possible."

The duo recruited another friend who was also a mama and ecstatic to have a kid-free day on the trail. But once her team was assembled, Chelsea had to address another component of the adventure: mom guilt at leaving *her* children behind.

Chelsea will be the first to say it: Her two daughters are her world. As a stay-at-home mom, Chelsea's life revolves around her kids and she wouldn't have it any other way. She began hiking with them when both girls were very young, so the trio frequently enjoyed trail time together while Chelsea's husband worked. As a mother, Chelsea believes her responsibility is to show her daughters what is possible for strong Black women, and that includes exposing them to all forms of outdoor recreation. Besides, she truly enjoys every moment with her girls and admits that she struggles leaving them.

"As a stay-at-home mom, you'd think I would feel smothered from being with children all day long, but it's the opposite: I feel terrible when I have fun without them," she shares.

As the day drew closer for her Wedge Mountain excursion, Chelsea battled major mom guilt. She had been on many hikes without her daughters before, but this hike would be the longest she had left them at home. She knew they would have a great day with their father, but she couldn't help but feel like she was selfish in doing something fun without them. Still,

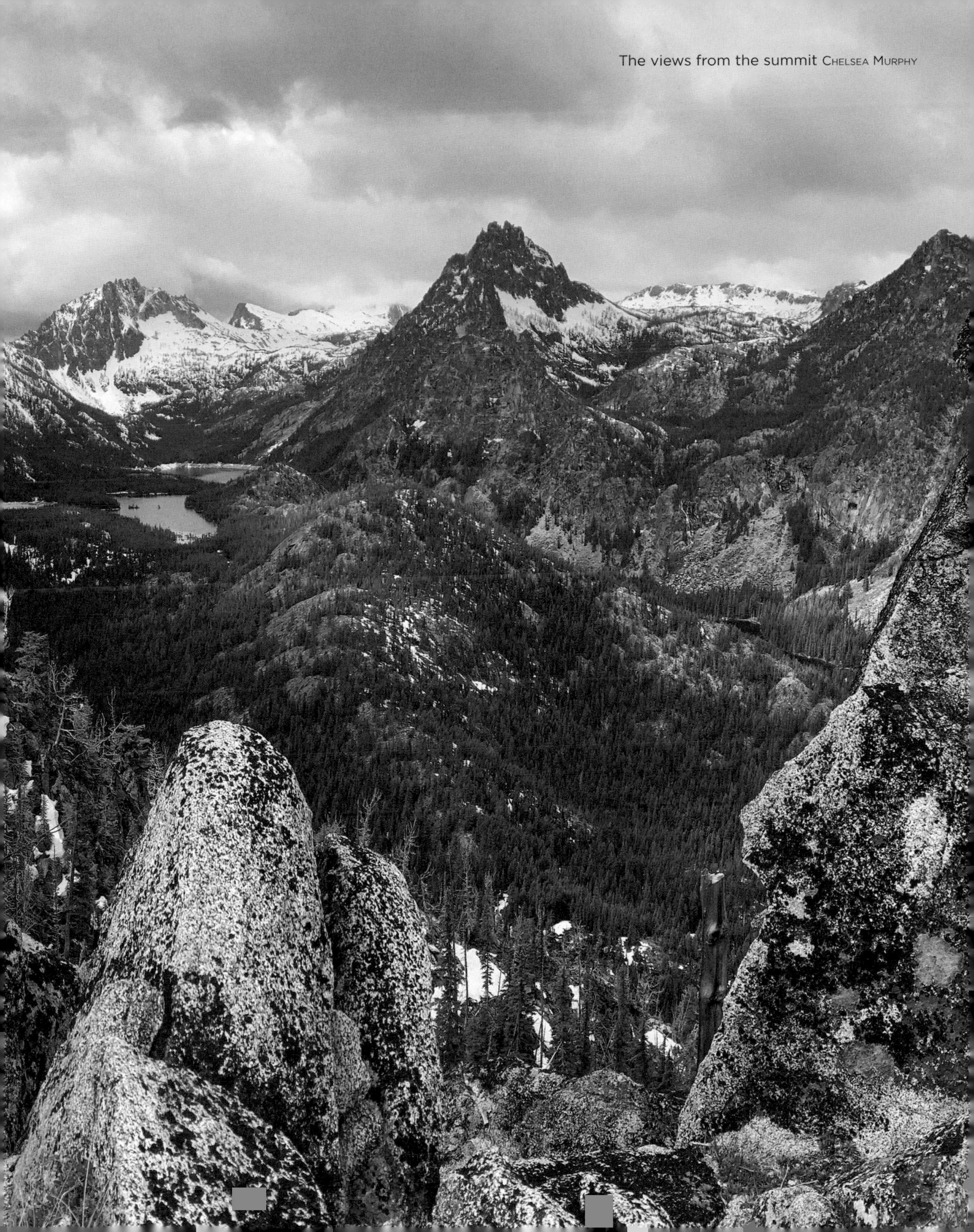

The views from the summit CHELSEA MURPHY

Chelsea knew that she needed to tackle Wedge for herself. On the morning of the hike, she loaded up her gear and headed out the door with deep feelings of regret. As she met up with her two friends, she remembers thinking, "I don't deserve this."

But mom guilt often sits similarly to New Year's resolutions on going to the gym: Once you get out the door, it feels a lot easier. As the women began hiking the road together, the burden of guilt gradually lifted and Chelsea realized how fortunate she was to be enjoying this adventure with her friends.

"There we were: a Black girl who has never gone the distance; a girl so stoked to walk on the land and break free from her kids for a day; and a Leavenworth local needing to validate this myth of a hike," she says. "We were all on this trip together but for very different reasons. And that was kind of an amazing thing."

The women climbed through the morning, first along the dirt road and then into the high alpine where vivid flowers and fat succulents grew out of the rocks as if they had been cultivated by a master gardener. With each intentional step into the sky, Chelsea felt her feelings of guilt slip away. She absorbed snapshots of the scenery to share with her daughters later. She smiled as she thought of the fun her eldest would have on this trail, but accepted her gratitude that she alone was here today. By the time

A happy Chelsea after finally realizing her goal! Chelsea Murphy

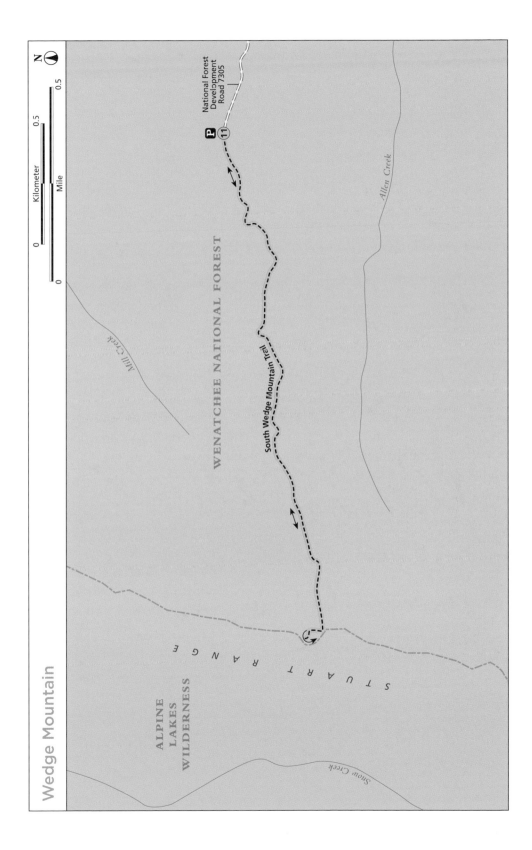

Wedge Mountain

N

Kilometer
0   0.5   0.5

Mile
0   0.5

National Forest
Development
Road 7305

P 11

WENATCHEE NATIONAL FOREST

South Wedge Mountain Trail

Allen Creek

Mill Creek

Snow Creek

ALPINE
LAKES
WILDERNESS

STUART RANGE

she walked over the rolling shoulder and found her friends waiting, Chelsea's smile was larger than life. She let out a holler of celebratory joy as she marveled at the vista beneath her feet.

Diaphanous lakes peppered the view below, each one glittering a new shade of aqua. Dark, stormy clouds sat trapped miles away, pouring deep gray raindrops into the Enchantments while Chelsea looked on from the sun-speckled summit of Wedge. A bead of sweat rolled down her brow as she looked on at the marvelous world before her and admired the cornucopia of colors that only Mother Nature could construct. Her feet ached and her shoulders screamed from the weight of her pack, but she felt immense pride at accomplishing her goal.

And she couldn't wait to share the adventure with her girls when she got home.

THE HIKE

Because this hike is more of a social trail, a GPS is highly recommended to navigate the path, particularly for the scramble back down to your car. Begin your hike by starting up the road, which eventually turns into a narrow path. There are two trails when you hit the horse camp/corral. You will continue through the camp and not to your left (this trail brings you to a collapsed tin-roofed cabin). Continue up to the ridge but be mindful of where you step. It's a bit of a scramble up to the top of the ridge, but once you're there you'll see for miles into the Enchantments, including the beauty of Snow Lake. If you go first thing in the morning, the sun will illuminate the Enchantments, but if you go later in the day you'll be staring into the sun while on the ridge. Retrace your steps back to the trailhead.

MILES AND DIRECTIONS

0.0 Begin hiking at the unnamed trailhead at the following GPS coordinates: N47 29.934' / W120 41.376'.

0.7 Intersect with the horse camp/corral. Continue through the camp.

1.2 Trail opens out into an old burn area with downed logs. Make sure to follow the most obvious trail.

1.5 Reach the ridge and spectacular views. Retrace your steps back to your car.

3.0 Arrive back at the trailhead.

BROOKE MURRAY

Mount Timpanogos via Aspen Grove Trail
Alpine, Utah

Brooke Murray is a 35-year-old mama with one mantra: motherhood with a side of dirt. In a former life, she worked in human genetics research in Utah, but her world flipped upside down with the arrival of her son, Huck. She soon found herself a single mother embarking on a career change in an effort to reconstruct a new life for her baby. She began using social media (mainly Instagram) to collaborate with outdoor brands to encourage families to get outside. Through these partnerships, Brooke was able to build a new career while also spending more time with Huck.

Now Brooke has a second child—her daughter, Tatum—with her husband, Patton, and they live in Colorado. She is the cofounder of WildKind, a digital membership community designed to educate and empower families to find their wild.

Brooke Murray Brooke Murray

While it isn't the tallest peak in the state or even the grandest in the Wasatch Mountains, Mt. Timpanogos has an allure that is all its own. Mt. Timp (as locals call it) is the most popular hike in Utah for good reason. Cascading waterfalls and a cornucopia of flower-filled meadows are just two of the beautiful sights to behold along the Aspen Grove Trail. This route can be crowded and it is rare to find solitude, but there is a silver lining: You've never seen so many mountain goats.

Nearest town: Orem

Getting there: For visitors entering from Provo on 189 North, take a left on Route 92. Follow this road for 4 miles past Sundance Resort. You will see the Aspen Grove parking lot on the left side just after the fee station.

Trailhead: Aspen Grove Trailhead

GPS: N40 24.264' / W111 36.258'

Fees and permits: $6 day-use fee or free for annual National Park Pass holders. Back-country camping is free.

Trail users: Hikers, trail runners, backpackers

Elevation gain: 5,377 feet

Length: 15.8 miles (out-and-back)

Approximate hiking time: Full day or overnight

Difficulty: Strenuous

Seasonal highlights: Due to its lush, alpine location, Mt. Timpanogos has some of the best displays of wildflowers in early August. Keep your eyes peeled on your way up: Mountain goats are known to romp around on the cliffs.

Managing agency: US Forest Service–Uinta-Wasatch-Cache National Forest

EXPERIENCING IT

The year 2015 was not going to plan. In fact, Brooke Murray felt like her entire world had hopped off its axis and begun spiraling faster than the teacups at Disney World. With the ink still wet on her divorce papers, Brooke was realizing that the year would look a lot different than she had expected. Instead of navigating the summer months with her partner as they dealt with diaper blowouts and middle-of-the-night feedings, she was learning how to become a strong single mother for her son, Huck. Instead of

Soaking in the views with a little Huck on her back Brooke Murray

holing up in her bedroom sobbing all day while mourning the loss of her previous life, Brooke was mentally fortifying herself to become the pillar she knew her son needed.

No, 2015 was not going to plan. But if anyone could roll Brooke's world back onto its axis, it was Mother Nature.

Mt. Timpanogos dominates the northeast side of the Utah Valley with its impressive stature and towering altitude. At a whopping 11,749 feet, Timpanogos is the second-highest peak in the Wasatch Mountains. Thanks to the curious mountain goats and brightly colored wildflowers peppering the landscape, Timp is a perennial favorite for hikers and backpackers wanting to test their physical mettle. Brooke was no different.

For the past 5 years, Timp had been her metaphorical yardstick for physical fitness. Each year, Brooke would tackle the peak from the Aspen Grove Trail, jogging a bit of the way before tagging the summit and returning to her car in an easy backpacking trip. She typically flew through the route because her pre-motherhood fitness allowed her to easily cover the 16 miles and 5,400 vertical feet of gain. The annual pilgrimage to Timp was never daunting and it was always worth it.

BACKPACKING WITH BABIES

You may feel like "backpacking with babies" is a typo, but it isn't! It is possible to embark upon grand outdoor adventures with babies as long as you are adequately prepared for your time in the wild. Here are a few tips to get you started.

- *Start young.* It's scary to think about sleeping in a small tent with a baby when you can't even get her to sleep in a climate-controlled room at home, but here's the secret: Babies will adapt to anything. If your babe learns about life in a tent from an early age, it will be a lot easier as she grows older—and more mobile.
- *Ditch the cotton.* Just like with adults, you don't want to dress your babe in cotton. Cotton holds a lot of moisture so it will absorb every single drop of your child's perspiration, holding the dampness next to her skin. It can be tricky to find non-cotton onesies, but they are out there.
- *Use sun protection.* Speaking of onesies, don't forget to pack extras for those non-sleep hours. Regardless of whether your baby is in a front-carrier or a backpack kid carrier, his legs and arms will be exposed to Mother Nature—and that includes his feet. By wearing a long-sleeved onesie with feet, you are protecting his extremities from the powerful UV rays.
- *Mimic your at-home sleep routine.* For most parents, bedtime is the scariest barrier: How will your child sleep in a tent? To make the transition as seamless as possible, do your best to simulate your at-home routine. If you use white noise at home, put a white noise app on your phone. If she has a stuffy that she sleeps with, pack that puffy friend along on the journey. (What's 5 more ounces at this point, you know?) The more she has to remind her of home, the easier it will be on everyone.
- *Practice safe(r) sleep.* Keeping your baby warm at night is daunting, but it is possible to do without adding a bunch of loose layers. There is at least one infant-specific 20-degree sleeping bag on the market, making this process a breeze. If you can't spring for a tiny sleeping bag, consider investing in a warm snowsuit that your baby can also wear during the winter.

Brooke and Huck are all smiles in Utah's high country Brooke Murray

It was late August when she made the decision to take 7-month-old Huck up to Mt. Timpanogos. Camping held a special place in Brooke's heart and she wanted to share that same experience with him—even if she was doing it the hard way by launching straight into a tough backpacking trip. Beyond the outdoor education, Brooke also knew this trip was important for an entirely different reason.

"I needed to know I was still meeting this personal goal, even after having my son," she remembers. "It felt special to hang onto that part of me."

In preparation, Brooke spent a few days planning the trip. First, she decided on a route. Emerald Lake sits at 10,393 feet and is roughly 5 miles into the hike. She decided that would be her base camp. Then she set about packing. Huck still nursed so his food and hydration were covered. The twosome would share a sleeping bag, so she focused on extra layers and diapers for her son. As she threw everything together, she vividly remembers thinking that it was "only an extra 15 pounds. I've got this."

But Mt. Timpanogos doesn't pull any punches: Hikers begin climbing from the parking lot and they don't stop until they reach the summit. Having day hiked this same route many times before, Brooke thought that getting to the lake would be a *mellow* journey. She envisioned arriving at camp with ample time to pitch the tent and enjoy a warm meal before the glowing orb dipped below the horizon and plunged the basin into dark shadows.

As with many things in 2015, the day didn't go as planned.

Almost immediately after leaving the trailhead, Brooke realized her journey would be more challenging than she expected. Huck popped his first tooth the night before, leaving her happy baby with a painful mouth and a day full of audible fussing that never stopped. And Brooke was tired. While nursing made it easy to feed Huck on the go, she underestimated the amount of calories and energy she needed to sustain both her son and herself. As she climbed higher and higher into the sky, she felt her enthusiasm waning. Her mind became her biggest obstacle and it continually tried to convince her to turn around.

"I can go back and get a burger and be happy," she remembers thinking. *"No one cares if you turn around. You don't have to prove anything to anyone else, so who cares if you don't make it?"*

But deep down inside, Brooke knew that she was the only person who really cared. She needed to make it to the lake so she could spend the night with Huck under the moonlit sky. She needed to make it to the lake so that she could prove to herself that 2015 had not extinguished her fire.

So she kept going. One hour rolled into 3, and 3 turned into 5. By the time she deliriously stumbled up to Emerald Lake, the temperature had dropped 50 degrees and darkness had fallen. Yet she made it. Maybe she wouldn't be summiting Mt. Timp the following morning, but that didn't matter. This was a victory.

Mt. Timpanogos was the first of many backpacking and camping and hiking trips that Brooke would enjoy with Huck, and then Patton, and then Tatum. And while she certainly didn't realize it at the time, Timp was simply a microcosm of her larger narrative and of what she wanted her future to hold.

"Being a single mom was never something I imagined for myself, but it gave me the opportunity to write my own story," Brooke says. "I was really trying to define who I was and what type of mom I wanted to be while we were on that hike. I think that gave me a little bit of fuel in the tank to work harder and keep that part of myself alive. This was my chance to create a purposeful life."

THE HIKE

Begin your hike at the Aspen Grove Trailhead located at the Theater-in-the-Pines picnic area. Bring a water filter on this trail since you'll come upon many creek crossings

Taking in the scenery with the early morning light Brooke Murray

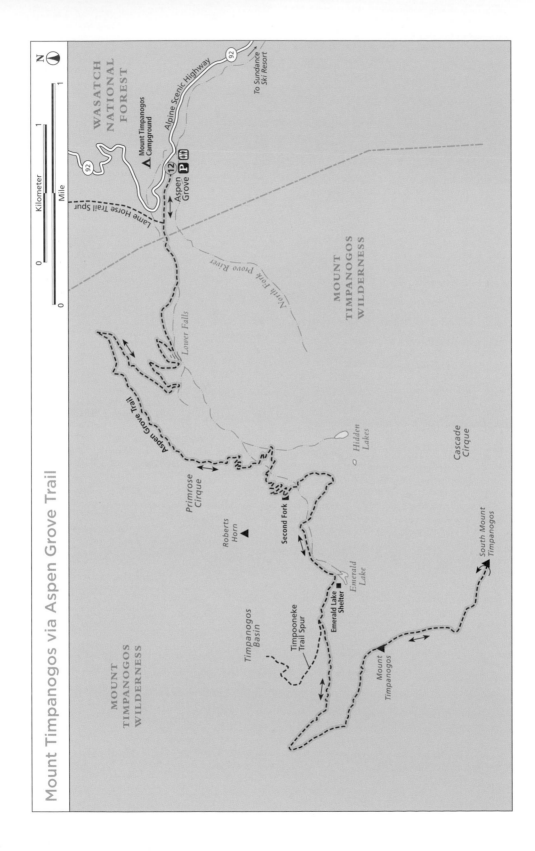

Mount Timpanogos via Aspen Grove Trail

N

Kilometer
0   1
Mile
0   1

WASATCH NATIONAL FOREST

92

Mount Timpanogos Campground

Alpine Scenic Highway

To Sundance Ski Resort

92

12

Aspen Grove

P

Lame Horse Trail Spur

North Fork Provo River

Lower Falls

MOUNT TIMPANOGOS WILDERNESS

Aspen Grove Trail

Primrose Cirque

Roberts Horn

Second Fork

Hidden Lakes

Cascade Cirque

Timpanogos Basin

Timpooneke Trail Spur

Emerald Lake Shelter

Emerald Lake

Mount Timpanogos

South Mount Timpanogos

MOUNT TIMPANOGOS WILDERNESS

and other water sources for you to fill up your water bladder. The trail starts as a gradual climb, but after the first waterfall crossing, it steeply ascends through a series of switchbacks up the Primrose Cirque. It isn't until you reach mile 4 that the trail lets up and your legs (and lungs!) can get a break from the ascent. Be on the lookout for wildflowers galore! The surrounding landscape is chock-full of lupines, penstemons, forget-me-nots, and the unique elephanthead lousewort (the flower petals look like elephants' trunks). You'll skirt by Emerald Lake, which is a great spot to replenish your depleted water bladder and grab a quick snack before the final few miles up to the summit. You'll reach the saddle of the summit and only be a mere 20 minutes from the top. Snap some photos at the graffiti-covered shelter at the top and then make your way back down the same way you came in.

MILES AND DIRECTIONS

0.0 Begin hiking at the Aspen Grove Trailhead at the Theater-in-the-Pines picnic area.

1.0 The first of many waterfalls along the trail.

1.2 Begin steeply ascending the switchbacks within the Primrose Cirque.

3.0 Enter a boulder field, and be aware that rock slides can occur.

3.2 Second set of steep switchbacks heading up the Primrose Cirque.

4.4 Trail levels out for a bit of a reprieve.

5.2 Emerald Lake.

6.3 Timpooneke Trail meets up with the Aspen Grove Trail.

7.9 Summit of Mount Timpanogos. Return the way you came.

15.5 Arrive back at the trailhead.

13

JENNIFER PHARR DAVIS

Petroglyph Canyon Trail
Valley of Fire State Park, Nevada

It is not hyperbole to say that Jennifer Pharr Davis is one of the greatest long-distance hikers of all time. Born and raised in Hendersonville, North Carolina, Jennifer did

Jennifer Pharr Davis with her daughter, Charley JENNIFER PHARR DAVIS

not grow up hiking or camping or backpacking. However, after her 2005 graduation from Alabama's Samford University, Jennifer decided to thru-hike (hike the entire distance in one trip) the 2,190-mile Appalachian Trail (AT). It changed her life. From that point forward, Jennifer knew what she wanted from life and pursuing outdoor adventure was a large component.

Since that first thru-hike on the AT, Jennifer's list of accolades has grown significantly. She has been National Geographic's Adventurer of the Year and an ambassador for the American Hiking Society. To date, she has hiked over 15,000 miles on long trails around the world including thru-hikes on the Pacific Crest Trail, the Colorado Trail, Europe's Tour du Mount Blanc, Scotland's West Highland Way, and the GR 20 in Corsica. But she is perhaps most well-known for her three thru-hikes of the AT. On one of those trips in 2011, Jennifer set the fastest known time (FKT) for men and women by completing the entire Appalachian Trail in 46 days, 11 hours, and 20 minutes. This amounted to an average of 47 miles per day, and the record stood until 2015 when Scott Jurek completed the journey 3 hours and 12 minutes faster.

Today, Jennifer lives in Asheville, North Carolina, with her husband, 8-year-old daughter, Charley, and 4-year-old son, Gus. Jennifer still hikes but is also an author, speaker, and business owner of her guiding company, Blue Ridge Hiking Company.

Who would've thought that just an hour's drive from Las Vegas lies one of the most geologically unique landscapes in the entirety of the United States?! One of many trails within the Valley of Fire State Park is Petroglyph Canyon, a short hike enjoyed by all ages and all skill levels. It is one of the easiest trails from which to see an abundance of petroglyphs, which means it's also usually busy. It's best to see this trail early in the morning or just before sunset, when the light bounces off the red rock canyon walls and the heat of the day has long since passed (120 degrees in the summertime is considered "normal" here).

Nearest town: Las Vegas

Getting there: For visitors entering the Valley of Fire State Park from Las Vegas, take I-15 north for 32 miles. Take exit 75 toward Valley of Fire/Lake Mead and keep left to merge onto Valley of Fire Highway. After 18 miles, take a left onto Mouse's Tank Road toward the Valley of Fire Visitor Center. In 1 mile, the parking lot will be on your right.

Trailhead: Mouse's Tank Trailhead

GPS: N36 26.466' / W114 30.996'

Fees and permits: Day users pay a $10 fee.

Trail users: Hikers, history buffs, archaeologists

Elevation gain: 55 feet

Length: 0.8 mile (out-and-back)

Approximate hiking time: Quarter of a day

Difficulty: Easy

Seasonal highlights: Due to its southern desert location, Valley of Fire State Park is best visited from September to May. Summer months carry extremely high temperatures considered dangerous and hikes should never be attempted during the middle of the day.

Managing agency: Nevada State Parks–Valley of Fire State Park

EXPERIENCING IT

Jennifer Pharr Davis has hiked all over the world, covering more distance and elevation gain than most humans experience in their lives. She ran 47 miles per day for 46 consecutive days on the Appalachian Trail. She trekked 522 miles with 128,000 feet of elevation change on Spain's GR 11 while in her second trimester of pregnancy with Charley. She hiked North Carolina's 1,175-mile Mountains-to-Sea Trail all while nursing her newborn son, Gus.

Yes, it's fair to say that Jennifer has experienced grander adventures than many will ever undertake. But on one dusty warm day in August 2014, her biggest adventure was watching her almost-2-year-old daughter roll around in the sand on the side of a 4-mile loop trail.

Seven years prior, Jennifer was crushing her hiking goals, specifically focusing on her successful FKT score of the Appalachian Trail. In 2008, she had first set the women's supported speed record by completing

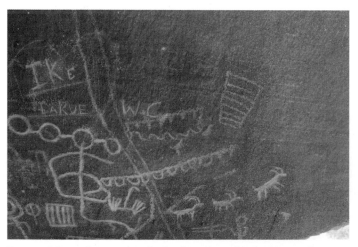
Some of the unique petroglyphs found on the canyon walls (mixed in with a little unfortunate vandalism) KATIE GARDNER

WHAT CAN'T JENNIFER DO?

Jennifer's career is so rich with milestones that it can be tough to keep her accolades straight. We broke down her hiking resume year by year so you can better understand how she managed to cover 14,000 miles on six continents. Here we go:

- 2005: Thru-hike (northbound) of the Appalachian Trail
- 2006: Summitted Mt. Kilimanjaro in Tanzania and thru-hiked the Pacific Crest Trail
- 2007: Machu Picchu and Cotahuasi Canyon in Peru along with the FKT on the 280-mile Long Trail in Vermont
- 2008: Self-supported FKT on Australia's 600-mile Bibbulmun Track, as well as the women's FKT on the AT (southbound)
- 2009: Thru-hiked the 480-mile Colorado Trail
- 2010: Thru-hiked the 80-mile Foothills Trail in South Carolina, the 110-mile GR 20 in Corsica, the 110-mile Tour du Mont Blanc in Europe, the 180-mile Pembrokeshire Coast Path in Wales, and the 95-mile West Highland Way in Scotland
- 2011: Set the new FKT on the AT
- 2012: Completed the 550-mile GR 11 in Spain and the 50-mile Laugavegur Trail in Iceland (while pregnant!)
- 2013: Day hiked in all 50 states with Brew and Charley while traveling the United States on her book tour
- 2014: Section-hiked a 250-mile section on the Continental Divide Trail
- 2015: Hiked the 100-mile Bartram Trail in North Carolina and another 250-mile section of the Continental Divide Trail in Wyoming
- 2016: Thru-hiked the 500-mile Camino de Santiago in Spain as well as summited Mt. Katahdin and Mount St. Helens while pregnant with her son, Gus
- 2017: Thru-hiked the 1,175-mile Mountains-to-Sea Trail while nursing Gus
- 2018: Completed the 300-mile Pinhoti Trail in Alabama
- 2019: Hiked the 300-mile Benton Mackaye Trail through Georgia, Tennessee, and North Carolina

the AT in 57 days, 8 hours, and 35 minutes. But she knew she had more in the tank and wanted to push her own boundaries. She wanted the overall speed record—not just the women's title—and 2011 was the year to do it. Over the course of those 46 days, Jennifer endured miserable diarrhea, battled through a sleet storm in New Hampshire's White Mountains, tolerated wildly painful shin splints, and ate

More of the petroglyphs that can be seen on the hike KATIE GARDNER

copious amounts of Nutella wraps all while establishing her new limits—and the overall FKT.

She could've gone after her speed record any old year, but Jennifer knew it was important to try in 2011. The Appalachian Trail has always been her favorite long hike and she thrived on the feeling of speedy weightlessness she experienced while hoofing through the rugged terrain. She wanted to tackle this goal unburdened from the weight of responsibility, especially because she knew her next chapter was a doozie: motherhood.

After Charley was born in fall 2012, Jennifer and Brew struggled to piece together their new life. Brew was a school teacher and Jennifer was always zipping around as she balanced her speaking and writing schedules with her guiding company. Stressed out and always moving in different directions, Jennifer says the twosome had "incompatible schedules" once they factored a child into the mix. Something needed to give and the family decided it was Brew's work at the school.

Simultaneously, Jennifer was prepping for a summerlong tour for her new book, *Called Again: A Story of Love and Triumph.* Once Brew quit teaching, the family had a lot more flexibility so they decided to tackle the tour together: Jennifer, Brew, and 6-month-old Charley. The concept was simple: Jennifer would move around the country, hosting various speaking engagements while also hiking in all fifty states. As a byproduct, this meant Charley would ultimately end up trekking paths in all of the states, too.

Days and weeks melted into months. Summer days faded into brisk fall mornings and chilly winter evenings. What was once planned to be a summerlong book tour turned into an 18-month cross-country zigzag filled with hiking, speaking engagements, and 24-hour-per-day family time. Jennifer laughs as she compares the tour to a thru-hike, joking that the space inside the family's Prius was comparable to a three-person tent and that the adults wore the same outfits daily, just like thru-hikers. But beyond the daily grind involved in bopping around the country, Jennifer and her family also experienced a new version of trail magic.

In the thru-hiking community, trail magic is an unexpected gift or occurrence that raises the hiker's spirits. Sometimes, it takes the form of a beautiful moose crossing the path in front of you.

Charley treating the desert like her own personal beach
JENNIFER PHARR DAVIS

Other times, it's a random lemonade stand set up on the side of the road or a box of candy bars on a front porch specifically for thru-hikers. Jennifer found trail magic on her "thru-hiker" book tour by strengthening her bond with Brew and Charley. Day after day, the threesome lived together, increasing their communication and finding

Jennifer and Charley celebrating the conclusion of their fifty-state hiking tour
JENNIFER PHARR DAVIS

daily inside jokes that only the family could understand. It wasn't lemonade or candy bars, but the familial ties formed were certainly a type of magic.

As the seasons ticked by and the book tour launched into its second year, Charley racked up quite a hiking resume. By the time Jennifer and her family reached Valley of Fire State Park in Nevada, Charley was closing in on her second birthday and the tour was wrapping up in its fiftieth state. To ring in her daughter's monumental accomplishment, Jennifer opted for the Petroglyph Canyon Trail.

The mildly undulating path is nothing like the trails that Jennifer had tackled in her past FKT attempts, but it was perfect for Charley. As the family sauntered toward the petroglyphs, the little girl intrinsically noticed the sand surrounding the area. Of course, her 2-year-old eyes didn't see it as "sand on the side of the trail." Instead, this

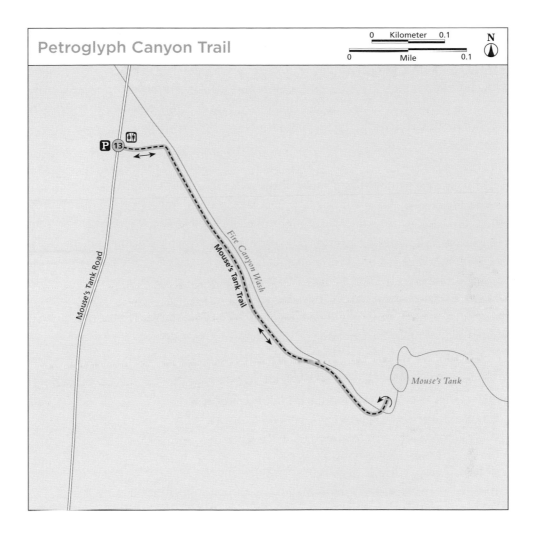

Petroglyph Canyon Trail

0   Kilometer   0.1

0   Mile   0.1

N

Mouse's Tank Road

Fire Canyon Wash

Mouse's Tank Trail

P 13

Mouse's Tank

was a next-level sandbox that she was eager to dive into! Charley immediately flopped into the toasty granules, heated by the high Nevada sunshine. Unlike other sandboxes, the desert doesn't have any barrier walls so Charley rolled back and forth, giggling while the sand slid down the back of her shirt and filled her pants. As far as she was concerned, this desert beach was the best thing she'd ever encountered.

Jennifer stood on the trail, a mere half mile from the parking lot, watching her daughter enthusiastically frolic on the ground. She thought back to 2 years prior and remembered the nervousness she had felt about launching into motherhood. Even though she yearned to be a mother, she remembers the feelings of fear and hesitation while wondering how parenting would or could change outdoor adventure. But as she watched Charley spin around in the sand, she acknowledged all the trails she had hiked with her daughter over the course of the past 18 months. Some were short and many were slow, but the family had experienced more varied scenery and terrain than Jennifer had witnessed in all of her FKT attempts.

In that moment, she felt a fullness unlike any other she had ever experienced. She knew this was symbolic of many things. But above all else, she saw the message clearly: Adventure was still possible with her children by her side. It may look and feel different, but it's just as rich—and even sweeter.

THE HIKE

Begin your hike at the Mouse's Tank Picnic Area (parking is limited so come early or wait for a spot). Although this is a short hike with minimal elevation gain, bring plenty of water as you will soon find out that the hot Nevada sun quickly heats up the canyon walls. Almost immediately, you'll see petroglyphs on the canyon walls. There are four areas where there is an abundance of petroglyphs but they can also be spotted throughout the entire hike. The end of the hike brings you to Mouse's Tank, which is a small body of water within the canyon holes that have been carved out over time. Enjoy a quick snack and then head back the way you came. Keep an eye out for petroglyphs you may have missed!

MILES AND DIRECTIONS

0.0 Begin hiking at the Mouse's Tank Picnic Area.

0.1 First petroglyphs on a canyon wall can be seen.

0.2 Second set of petroglyphs can be seen.

0.25 Third bunch of petroglyphs can be seen.

0.35 Last area with an abundance of petroglyphs.

0.4 Arrive at Mouse's Tank (small body of water within the canyon ruts). Return the way you came.

0.8 Arrive back at the trailhead.

14

SHON'T SAVAGE

Shi Shi Beach
Neah Bay, Washington

Shon't Savage goes by a lot of titles: public health project program manager, life partner, wild spirit, board member, calming soul, and mother, to name a few. This Seattle-
based outdoor mama first discovered the rejuvenating powers of the outdoors over

Shon't Savage SHON'T SAVAGE

a decade ago after enduring a painful divorce. While sharing custody of her now-13-year-old son, Sam (or The Dude, as Shon't affectionately nicknamed him), this 46-year-old found herself with surplus free time. To avoid the emptiness in her home, she hit the trails and discovered a new love. These days, she enjoys hiking, backpacking, camping, and mountain climbing, both in the Pacific Northwest and internationally.

As a board member of the nonprofit Adventure Mamas, Shon't is a firm believer in maternal wellness and empowerment. She proudly encourages mothers to prioritize their own mental and physical health in an effort to better support their families. To this end, Shon't frequently embarks upon solo adventures to replenish her soul and maintain her individuality.

Enjoyed as a moderate day hike or a peaceful overnight backpacking trip, Shi Shi Beach (pronounced "Shy Shy" and not "Shee Shee") is arguably the crown jewel of both Olympic National Park and the Makah Indian Reservation (the beach is located in the park but the trailhead is on the reservation). The slightly undulating trail is frequently muddy and wet thanks to the copious amounts of precipitation inherent in the Pacific Northwest's coastal forest. But once the route descends down to the pristine sandy beach and rugged coastline packed with windswept campsites and glistening tidepools, you'll only remember the awe-inspiring scenery.

Nearest town: Neah Bay

Getting there: For visitors entering Neah Bay from the east on Route 112, take a left on Backtrack Road. Follow this road for 1.7 miles until it turns into Makah Passage. Keep going for another 3.7 miles as the road eventually runs along the ocean. Then take a right on Tsoo-Yess Beach Road where you will continue for roughly 2 miles. You will see overnight parking on the left side.

Trailhead: Shi Shi Beach Trailhead

GPS: N48 17.622' / W124 39.906'

Fees and permits: Backpackers need both a Makah Recreation Pass ($10) and a Wilderness Permit ($8 per person per night plus a $6 fee) for Olympic National Park. Reservations are required May–September.

Trail users: Hikers, trail runners, backpackers

Elevation gain: 585 feet

The mystical waters of Shi Shi Beach
WILL ROCHFORT

Length: 6.6 miles (out-and-back)

Approximate hiking time: Full day or overnight

Difficulty: Moderate

Seasonal highlights: Due to its northern location, the best time to visit Shi Shi Beach is April through September when the daytime temps are warm and the evenings are pleasant. Keep your eyes peeled: Bald eagles have been known to circle campers on the beach.

Managing agency: National Park Service–Olympic National Park and Makah Indian Reservation

EXPERIENCING IT

"Hey mom, do you remember that time when I got mad at you in my bedroom?"
"Mom, can we talk about what happened at school last month?"
"What type of bird has white feathers like that, mom?"
"Mama, what's the difference between a sea urchin and an anemone?"

It was a classic summer day in the Pacific Northwest. Thick, gray clouds hung low on the horizon as weakened sunrays poked through the gaps, beckoning The Dude to run and play amidst the sugar-like sand on Shi Shi Beach. Cool, salty air filled Shon't's nostrils as she inhaled a breath of gentle ocean wind and exhaled all of life's problems left back in Seattle. She watched as her 12-year-old son scampered along the frothy sea foam line left behind by the retreating ocean waves and peered into the animated tide pools packed with marine life. Shon't smiled. She knew her son's laundry list of questions signified more than simply curiosity, and she was here for it.

A lot can change in a decade.

It had been more than 10 years since Shon't first discovered the rejuvenating powers of Mother Nature. Divorce is never easy but it can be necessary and Shon't found herself on the right end of the first day of a new life. But adjusting to her future took practice and Shon't needed to learn a lot about one person: herself. She looked in the mirror and couldn't recognize who she saw. She had abandoned vital elements core to her being, fusing her identity with her marriage. She realized she needed to do two things: find and re-create herself. But saying those words aloud was a lot easier than actually doing it.

Plus, she was lonely. Thanks to shared custody, her 2-year-old son spent a lot of time with his father, leaving Shon't's home empty and alone. Without the pitter-patter of toddler feet and infectious giggles to fill the hallways, Shon't knew she needed to fill the void with something that would also replenish her soul. So she started hiking.

"Hiking was my space; that was my therapy outside of therapy," she remembers.

Sam (The Dude) cruising toward camp SHON'T SAVAGE

Her self-healing trajectory connected her with a myriad of strong outdoor women who offered guidance, and Shon't's innate curiosity carried her through a number of experiences. She learned to spend solo time hiking and backpacking, marveling at the mental conversations she enjoyed by herself. Through her induction to the outdoor world, Shon't rediscovered who she was while shifting the narrative about who she could be. She learned about a grander world and eagerly stepped foot into it, excited at what she would discover.

Knowing that adventure had brought such joy and awareness into her life, Shon't was confident that it would play a part in her son's life, too. While The Dude began hiking at an early age, he had yet to try backpacking. As he grew older, Shon't felt like he was ready to experience one of her favorite things: sleeping in the wild. So they researched the route, packed their backpacks, and hopped in the car to drive to Neah Bay.

They were merely 20 minutes into the hike when Shon't knew it was a good decision. As the mother-son duo ambled through the Sitka spruces, The Dude began peppering the silence with intermittent bursts of conversation. For some adolescents, this may be the norm, but it was strikingly noticeable to Shon't because Sam has dyslexia. As she describes it, "his brain is beautifully wired to see the world in a different way, but sometimes it is hard for him to process and regurgitate that in a way we can understand." As a result, it's often easier for The Dude to communicate with other individuals with a machine or a screen—not words.

But at Shi Shi, Sam was full of conversation. At first, the topics started small and he asked about various wildlife in the area. As the minutes ticked by, he opened up more. He

Shon't with her son, The Dude SHON'T SAVAGE

The Dude playing near the water SHON'T SAVAGE

began questioning his mom about personal conversations and inquiries about why things were the way they were. As they descended the steep hillside toward the beach, The Dude asked about events from the past month, questioning logic and seeking rationality behind what happened. Shouldering a heavy pack but feeling light from conversation, Shon't trudged through the sand alongside her son, watching him make space for himself that he somehow couldn't find back in the city.

With each subsequent query, Shon't learned a little bit more about Sam. He intentionally left silence after each question, almost as if he was offering it up to his mother for examination and reflection. This gave her pause to consider and respond, asking him about his feelings and why he felt the way he felt. It was a beautiful exchange, and certainly one that is all too infrequent with preteen children.

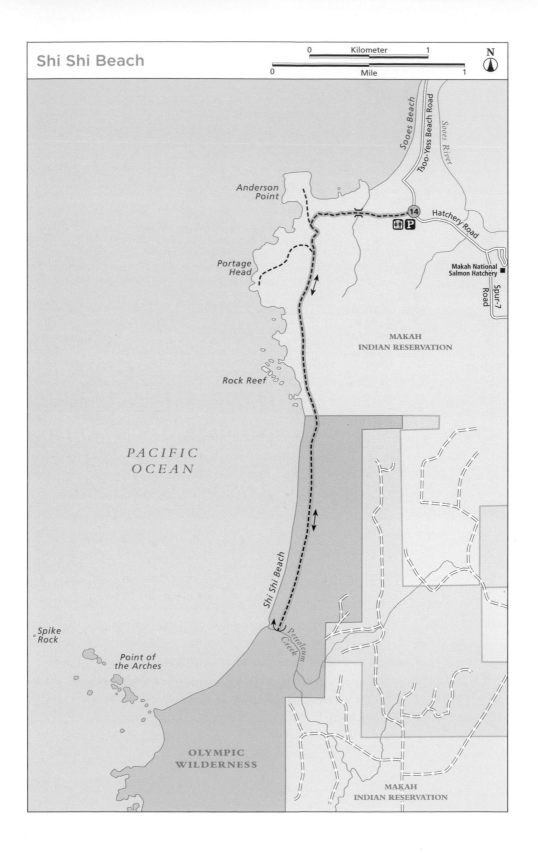

Shi Shi Beach

Anderson
Point

Portage
Head

Rock Reef

*PACIFIC
OCEAN*

Spike
Rock

Point of
the Arches

*OLYMPIC
WILDERNESS*

Shi Shi Beach

Petroleum Creek

Sooes Beach

Tsoo-Yess Beach Road

Sooes River

14 Hatchery Road

Makah National
Salmon Hatchery

Spur-7
Road

MAKAH
INDIAN RESERVATION

MAKAH
INDIAN RESERVATION

0   Kilometer   1

0   Mile   1

N

And it continued throughout the weekend. At any given moment, Sam would come running to his mama, eager to ask her a question about a sea urchin or show her a weird piece of driftwood he found in the sand. Often, his discoveries would lead to further conversation, allowing Shon't to engage with her son in a new way every time. She watched The Dude run along the beach, freely moving without the limits or boundaries that apply back in civilization. And often, she joined him. They climbed up sea stacks together and flipped over rocks in tidepools to spot tiny fish or sea stars. On the last morning, she forwent packing up the tent in favor of running through the sand with Sam, chatting about how humans and the planet are all interconnected and codependent and how that applies to their everyday lives.

"I could see him processing, knowing what it was like to take up that space," Shon't says. "I watched him be in his body and take up that space and know that he'll be okay."

THE HIKE

Begin your hike at the Shi Shi Beach Trailhead near the fish hatchery on the Makah Indian Reservation. The trail heads west as it wraps through Sitka spruces and brushy clear-cut along a series of boardwalks and walkways. After roughly one mile, the path turns south and you'll definitely notice—because it gets messy almost immediately! The second mile slogs through classic coastal forest and the terrain is frequently muddy and wet. Remember: Prevent erosion by splashing directly through the puddles rather than widening the trail and walking around them. Then, tip over the edge of the bluffs and descend into Olympic National Park and down toward the sandy beach. Sand between your toes, head southward until you cross Petroleum Creek; this is where the campsites begin.

MILES AND DIRECTIONS

0.0 Begin hiking at the Shi Shi Beach Trailhead near the fish hatchery.

0.7 The trail turns southward and begins a brief climb into the coastal rainforest.

1.2 Begin steeply descending down the 150-foot bluff until it reaches the sandy beach.

2.1 Reach the bottom of the bluffs and begin trekking along the beach.

3.3 Cross Petroleum Creek and reach the beginning of the campsite zone. Retrace your steps back to the trailhead.

6.6 Arrive back at the trailhead.

ANGEL TADYTIN
Rainbow Bridge North Trail
Page, Arizona

Angel Tadytin is a 37-year-old Native American woman from the Navajo tribe, originally from Bitter Springs, Arizona, a small village near Page that is located in Navajo Nation. Born Many Goat for the Coyote Pass People, her maternal grandfather's clan is Bitterwater and her paternal grandfather's clan is Towering House. Professionally, Angel is a medical social worker who works with a home health and hospice agency to provide wraparound care for end-of-life hospice patients and at-home rehabilitation patients. Angel is an avid outdoorswoman who loves exploring the slot canyons and

Angel Tadytin and her husband, Darrin ANGEL TADYTIN

trails in the Southwest. She is an ambassador for Women Who Hike, frequently taking other women on hikes on the reservation while educating them on her cultural ancestry. To celebrate the one hundredth anniversary of Grand Canyon National Park, Teva also named her one of four "Faces of the Canyon," people whose lives were shaped by the magnificence of the Grand Canyon. Angel is also a mother to three children (ages 2, 9, and 14) and currently lives in Gilbert, Arizona, with her husband and kids.

Enjoyed safely as a multiday backpacking trip, Rainbow Bridge North Trail is something to behold. Considered to be the more scenic of the two trails to Rainbow Bridge, the north trail is longer but the reward is well worth it. The trail descends steeply into several canyons and across many creeks where remnants of past flash floods are easily seen. This is why it's best to only attempt this trail from March through mid-May and then not again until October through November. Although you can take a boat to see the Rainbow Bridge, it is not nearly as scenic or rewarding, so put in the sweat equity. A promise: You'll be rewarded.

Nearest town: Page, AZ

Getting there: For visitors entering from Page on Route 98, take a left onto Indian Road 16 North at Inscription House Trading Post turnoff. Take the paved road for 25 miles, after which it will turn to dirt. Once on the dirt road, take it for 5.4 miles to the Navajo Mountain Trading Post fork where you'll bear right and continue for another 8.5 miles to the trading post itself. Drive 3.7 miles past the trading post to a four-way intersection and continue straight. After 2.8 miles, take the fork in front of you to cross an earthen dam. Only 0.4 mile later, you'll bear left again at a fork. Travel 1.6 miles to Cha Canyon and park; the unmarked trailhead starts at the end of the road. A four-wheel-drive, high-clearance vehicle is required to reach the trailhead.

Trailhead: Rainbow Bridge North Trailhead

GPS: N37 05.010' / W110 47.754'

Fees and permits: Overnight permits are required ($12 per person per day) and must be obtained prior to your trip either by mailing a form or getting one in person at the Navajo Nation Parks and Recreation Department in Window Rock, AZ. Camping is not permitted within the Rainbow Bridge National Monument.

Trail users: Backpackers

Elevation gain: 5,593 feet

Length: 35 miles (out-and-back)

Approximate hiking time: Multiday backpacking

Difficulty: Strenuous

Seasonal highlights: Due to the trail's exposure and high risk for flash floods, this trail should only be hiked March through mid-May or October through November.

Managing agency: Navajo Nation Parks and Recreation and National Park Service

EXPERIENCING IT

If Angel Tadytin has learned anything from parenting, it's this: Children help their mothers see the world through fresh eyes.

As a lifelong backpacker, Angel and her husband have spent countless hours on the trails, both on the Navajo Nation and off. Her childhood on the reservation meant she spent her days playing with her friends outside during the high heat of the Arizona

Cameron and Tate, cheesing for the camera ANGEL TADYTIN

WHAT IS THE LONG WALK?

The Long Walk (also known as The Long Walk of the Navajo or The Long Walk to Bosque Redondo) refers to the forced removal of the Navajo people (Diné) from their homelands by the US government.

In the mid-1800s, the United States began concerted expansion efforts west of the Mississippi River. In 1848, the United States and Mexico signed the Treaty of Guadalupe Hidalgo, effectively ending the Mexican-American War and placing the land now known as Texas, New Mexico, Arizona, Colorado, Utah, Nevada, and California under the control of the US government. Much of this region was Navajo homeland, but the United States now considered the land their own. European Americans began settling in and around the Navajo territory, which ultimately led to numerous conflicts with the Navajo people on one side and the settlers or the US Army on the other. In response, Major James H. Carleton ordered a "scorched earth" resistance against the Diné people, led by Kit Carson, attempting to defeat the Navajo by burning villages, slaughtering livestock, and removing water sources. Forced into desperation, the Navajo had few options and surrendered. Beginning in January 1864, the government attempted a form of ethnic cleansing by removing the Native people from their land by forcing them to endure a long walk of 250–450 miles. The endpoint was called Bosque Redondo Reservation in New Mexico, but in reality it was a pseudo–internment camp. Many Diné died on the walk (some historians estimate upwards of 200 deaths per day) due to harsh conditions, cruel distances, and minimal (if any) support from the soldiers. Once they arrived at Bosque Redondo, more than 8,000 Navajo people were settled onto an area of 40 square miles. Moreover, Mescalero Apaches were also placed in the camp and the Comanche people raided it frequently. Due to inept management and a lack of supplies, Bosque Redondo was abandoned, concluding with the 1868 Treaty of Bosque Redondo. This treaty allowed the Navajo to return to a small portion of their homeland in Arizona and New Mexico with promises of basic services from the government. Thus, the Diné people began their Long Walk Home on June 18, returning to their land.

summer, returning home for dinner covered in the state's dusty Casa Grande soil. Now that she is an adult, Angel still favors time spent in the wild. She loves exploring the darkened nooks and crannies of Utah's canyon country and scampering along the gritty sandstone peppering the Arizona desert. During all of these adventures, she treats the voyage like most grown-ups: big miles, hard days, and the occasional grinder that leaves her practically falling into the tent with exhaustion.

But as any mother can attest to, those schedules simply don't work with children.

Sunset in the desert ANGEL TADYTIN

In 2017, Angel arrived at a decision: It was time to take her two children on their first-ever backpacking trip. While her youngest was not yet born, her eldest sons were both experienced with day hikes and had spent much of their younger lives on the trail. But backpacking was different. This time, each child would carry an actual pack with varying weight. And there would be no kid carrier; each boy would walk every single mile of the trail with his own feet.

Situated in the northern reaches of Navajo Nation, Rainbow Bridge National Monument is one of the most remote spots in the lower forty-eight states. Boasting one of the largest known natural bridges in the world, Rainbow Bridge cannot be reached

by vehicle. Instead, hikers must choose between two paths: the north trail or the south trail, with the northern route being both longer and more scenic. Knowing this, Angel opted for the Rainbow Bridge North route. Then, she got to work.

While Angel had backpacked the north trail previously, she admits that she didn't actually know much about the route. "I kinda put my head down and charged, logging 7 or 8 hours of hiking," she says. With her sons along for the ride, she wanted this trip to be different. She planned to tackle the 18-mile journey by splitting it up into three days and two nights, ensuring her boys did not hike more than 6 miles per day.

More importantly, she dove into research. In an effort to prepare herself for her children's predicted line of questioning, Angel read up on the geography of the region. She remembered visiting Rainbow Bridge in elementary school and learning that the massive structure was made by the wind and the water, so she opted to begin her lesson there. But in doing so, she found herself learning more about her ancestral history than she expected.

According to Angel, Navajo education is taught orally with elders verbally passing stories and information down to the younger generations. Typically, nothing is written. As a result, Angel says most of her inherited knowledge came from what her family chose to communicate with her. But as she continued researching the region, Angel learned more than she ever imagined.

"I already knew Navajo beliefs about how the bridge was made, but I learned how the Paiutes think it was made," she says. "It sits on the border of Arizona and Utah and three tribes inhabited that area. We all have different ideas about the history."

She dove into the stories, learning about the Paiute or Mountain Ute perspective alongside her own Navajo beliefs. She found one Navajo story that detailed how two

Following the stone path toward Rainbow Bridge
Angel Tadytin

boys wanted to cross the canyon but couldn't. They called upon the spirits and asked: *"How can we cross this?"* The spirits responded by building a big worm that solidified into stone so they could cross the canyon. Another Navajo story described two spirits who fell in love with each other from opposite sides of the abyss. They learned that the only way they could be together and touch each other was to live in a permanently solid state. But their love was so strong that they didn't care. They reached across the vast chasm and turned into stone, where they will spend time immemorial.

But not all of the ancestral memories conjured up during the backpacking trip were steeped in romanticism or friendly connections. As the Tadytin family continued into day 2 of their hike, the boys marveled at the towering canyon walls as they soared skyward.

"Mama, the walls are so cool!" Angel's eldest said. "How high do they go?"

In that moment, Angel seized upon the opportunity to teach her children an invaluable lesson about Navajo history.

"These walls aren't only pretty," she said. "They also mean safety. Our ancestors used these deep canyons to hide from soldiers so they didn't have to go on The Long Walk. Families would hide their children like you down here so they didn't get taken to boarding school."

The boys listened to the words of their mother as they trekked alongside the very canyon walls that hid their grandparents and great-grandparents from the US Army more than 150 years ago. While this was not a new conversation in the Tadytin family, it resonated differently this time. The children stared at the walls, perhaps envisioning the history that played out in a different century yet is still ingrained in modern life. They made the connection between their ancestors and this very location, deeply understanding the Native legends their mother had shared with them at home.

And when things got tough on the trail and their weary legs felt too exhausted to hike any farther, the boys continued to reference The Long Walk. As Angel and the children neared Rainbow Bridge, she saw her sons dramatically tiring and suggested a rest break. But they would hear none of it.

"I bet our family on The Long Walk was so strong that they could run this," her youngest son said. "We can do this. We're almost there!"

Soaking in the colorful scenery that is the Arizona desert ANGEL TADYTIN

THE HIKE

Begin your hike at the end of the road to start your descent into Cha Canyon on Navajo Nation land. Cha Canyon is the first of many canyons you'll go in and out of, which means an indefinite amount of ups and downs on your way to Rainbow Bridge. The second canyon is called Bald Rock and gives great views from the top. If you're finding that you are drinking your water at an alarming rate, make sure to fill up while you can. There are intermittent streams throughout the entire trail but water levels may be low depending on the season. A rule of thumb is to top up your water whenever you can! Next you'll cross N'asja Creek (which is usually flowing) before passing Owl Bridge. Remember to stay on the trail and do not climb up on any of the natural bridges you encounter. There is no water for 3 miles after Oak Canyon, so in case it hasn't been said enough, FILL UP ON WATER now. You'll eventually meet up with the south trail at which point you'll be close to your destination. Rainbow Bridge is a unique place that is sacred to many, so please respect all signs and stay on the trail. Enjoy the solitude of the landscape.

MILES AND DIRECTIONS

0.0 The trailhead starts at the end of the road.

1.0 Enter Cha Canyon where the creek is usually running.

3.5 Bald Rock Canyon campsite and intermittent creeks, depending on the season.

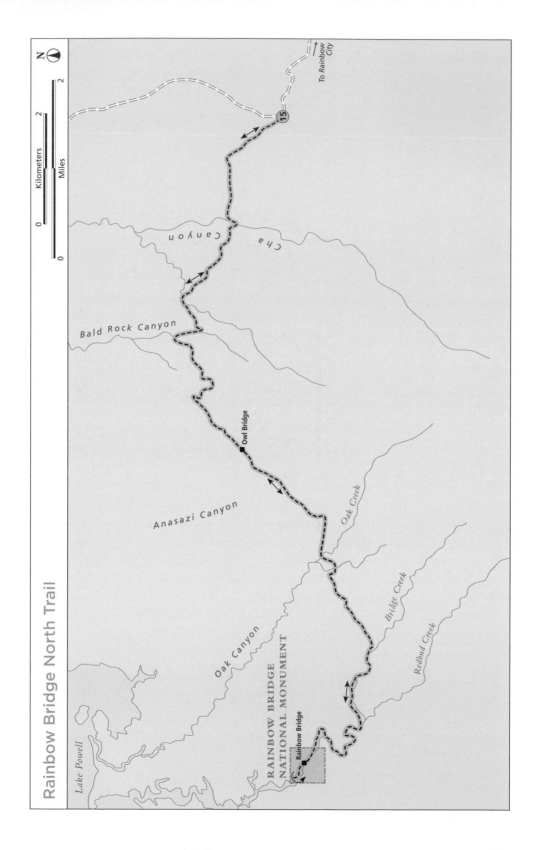

Rainbow Bridge North Trail

The Tadytin family after reaching the bridge ANGEL TADYTIN

5.0 Reach an old hogan (Navajo hut made from logs and earth), one of several you will see along the trail.

6.5 N'asja Creek campsite.

7.0 Pass an old sweat lodge and then you'll see Owl Bridge on your left (do not climb the bridge).

10.0 Enter Oak Canyon (there is no water after this for 3 miles).

11.5 Enter Bridge Canyon where it can become extremely hot from the canyon walls. Please be prepared with plenty of water prior to this spot.

15.0 Meet up with the south trail; water should be plentiful between several creeks. Fill up on water if you are low.

17.5 Rainbow Bridge. Retrace your steps back to your chosen campsite and eventually back out to the trailhead.

35.0 Arrive back at the trailhead.

JENNY TAYLOR

Goose Creek Falls Trail
McCall, Idaho

Jenny Taylor is the vice president of marketing in the Americas for outdoor brand Salomon. Founded in 1947 in Annecy, France, Salomon is currently the European leader in outdoor equipment while still maintaining a hefty foothold in the North American market with the brand's popular trail-running and skiing gear. Jenny has been with the brand for nearly 15 years, including the 2018 launch of the Salomon

Jenny Taylor DEREK TAYLOR

WMN campaign that sought to challenge stereotypes of women in the outdoors. To date, the project is the most-watched campaign in Salomon history with over 3.4 million views.

Jenny and her husband live in Huntsville, Utah, with their two children. Her eldest son, Hugo, is 8 and her youngest son, Kier, is 6. Jenny is an avid trail runner and the rest of the family frequently skis and mountain bikes, but hiking has been the common thread to keep them outside, no matter the occasion.

Tucked up near Brundage Mountain Resort, Goose Creek Falls epitomizes a hiker's delight. The turnaround point rewards visitors with a silvery cascade of water that plummets nearly 65 feet before gathering in a churning pool of whitewater froth. The trail is wildly popular—especially with families—so you won't find a ton of solitude. But that simply means you'll be able to make friends with those you meet on the trail. Bonus: Skip the summer crowds and visit during the fall when you can see the orange and yellow leaves along the path.

Nearest town: McCall

Getting there: From downtown McCall, head 5.6 miles northwest on Route 55 toward the Brundage Mountain Ski Resort. Turn right (north) onto Brundage Mountain Road. Continue driving for 3.4 miles until you see a snowmobile lot on the left side. This is the Gordon Titus Parking Area; park here. The trail begins at the north end of the parking lot.

Trailhead: Goose Creek Falls Trailhead

GPS: N44 59.391' / W116 11.343'

Fees and permits: None

Trail users: Hikers, trail runners

Elevation gain: 759 feet

Length: 3.0 miles (out-and-back)

Approximate hiking time: Half day

Difficulty: Easy-to-moderate

Seasonal highlights: This trail is a great option from spring until fall, but it truly shines during the warmest summer afternoons. Thanks to a dense canopy of Douglas fir, spruce, and pine trees, there is plenty of shade for little ones—and their parents.

Managing agency: Payette National Forest

EXPERIENCING IT

Some mamas are eager to hit the trail with their new babe, exemplifying a quick return to their former lives. Jenny Taylor was not one of them—and she'll be the first to admit that.

Born and raised in Pennsylvania, Jenny jumped into the outdoors from an early age. She attended Wyonegonic Camp when she was just a kid, and returned every year until college. Located on Moose Pond in Denmark, Maine, this all-girls international camp is the oldest program of its kind in the state and still offers young women the opportunity to learn "flexibility within a general structure." Jenny participated in wilderness trips, swimming lessons, archery, rock climbing, and horseback riding as she whiled away her summer days in the Pine Tree State. She loved Wyonegonic Camp so much that she spent her later teenage years as a camp counselor, advising and corralling the younger participants. In fact, Jenny still credits Wyonegonic with her subsequent decision to attend college in Vermont—another hub for outdoor recreation. This led to a string of jobs in the outdoor industry including ski resorts, outdoor clothing company Dakine, and now Salomon.

But then, she had children.

"Everyone told us, 'Don't change your lifestyle for your kids—just bring them with you!'" Jenny laughs. "Maybe I'm too much of a stress ball, but I could never do that."

Once Hugo and Kier (nicknamed Pancake) were born, Jenny admits that outdoor recreation changed. She hated skipping her children's naps and always worried that she would forget an important item like diapers or milk or even sunscreen for her baby's soft skin. As a self-described worrier, Jenny readily acknowledges that the stress of packing for four people took its toll; family adventure simmered for a few years.

But then, a small hike in Idaho in 2019 stoked the flames once again.

The Taylor family was nearing the end of their big summer road trip, wrapping up weeks of travel with a little time outside of McCall. After posting up at the nearby campground for a few nights, Jenny and her husband decided to tackle a family hike on the Goose Creek Falls Trail. Pancake was only 4 so the family packed along the trusty kid carrier like they had for nearly a decade.

Kier could walk on his own, of course. But his little legs lived in the in-between: long enough to cover distance but short enough that his parents never knew when he would tap out on the day's plans. They packed the kid carrier as insurance, knowing they could hoist him into the backpack when the hike became too tiring.

Cruising along at little-leg pace
DEREK TAYLOR

HOW TO CHOOSE A KID CARRIER

Hiking with children often requires a kid carrier, which may feel like a daunting task. Hopefully these tips make the buying process a little easier for you.

- *Evaluate your baby's neck strength.* If your baby cannot sit upright on her own, use a frameless front-carry that provides ample support. Once your child can sit upright and weighs at least 16 pounds, she is ready for a kid carrier.
- *Look for comfort.* If possible, purchase your kid carrier in a store where you (and anyone else who may carry the child) can try on the pack. Comfort is paramount because your pack load will only get heavier as your child grows!
- *Check sizing.* An adjustable back length is ideal if you are planning on sharing the work with another individual who is taller or shorter than you. This means you can both wear the same pack.
- *Consider purchasing accessories.* There are plenty of accessories to consider when shopping for a kid carrier, but here are a few of the most important:
  - *Sunshade:* to protect your child's skin
  - *Hip belt pockets:* great for snacks and car keys since they are accessible while hiking
  - *Hydration pockets or sleeve:* for water for both you and your child
  - *Kickstand:* stabilizes the kid carrier on uneven terrain
  - *Gear storage:* Most kid carriers have at least one stretchy mesh pocket and one zippered compartment. It's a good idea to evaluate how much storage you need before deciding on a backpack.
- *Check your child's comfort level.* Above all else, plop your kiddo inside "the cockpit" in the backpack before making the final decision. He will be spending a lot of time in there, so it's a good idea to make sure he likes his new space!

The family set out on the trail, immediately descending into the cool shade provided by the dense coniferous canopy above. Jenny's husband carried the unused kid carrier while she shouldered the snacks, water, and extra layers for the family. The kids scampered ahead, tripping in the dirt and jumping over the logs on the trail. Every bend in the path brought new squeals of excitement as the boys frolicked in the sunshine and explored nooks and crannies along the way. As the sun-drenched air warmed the sap in the surrounding pine trees, an intoxicating blend of lemon and musk wafted through the air and lingered in Jenny's nostrils. As her kiddos happily chattered ahead, she smiled with contentment. "Today is a good day," she thought to herself.

The key to successful hikes with younger children: snack breaks DEREK TAYLOR

The Taylor quartet kept hiking, pausing for every insect, wildflower, and blade of grass that caught the attention of Pancake or Hugo. But the sky was bluer than forget-me-nots and the clouds puffier than cotton balls, so Jenny and her family simply meandered toward Goose Creek without worrying over the trappings of daily conventions. They had no schedule, nowhere to be, and nothing to hurry their pace. Instead, they laughed and joked together while enjoying the bounty of Idaho's fresh air. In fact, it wasn't until the foursome reached the waterfalls and stopped for snacks that Jenny realized today's difference: Pancake wasn't in the kid carrier. He was still hiking on his own.

As she served the boys their lunch, Pancake walked over to the kid carrier and asked to sit in it while he scarfed down his sandwich. He climbed inside, using the fancy carrier as a glorified bench during the family's snack break.

"It was then that I realized he hadn't touched it the entire morning," Jenny remembers. "Here's my baby who always wanted to be carried, but it was like he decided to move on from that phase."

Often, hiking with kids calls for detailed negotiations. DEREK TAYLOR

After gulping down their food and water, Pancake and Hugo declared lunch to be over. Pancake climbed down from his kid carrier, brushed the sandwich crumbs from his shorts, and began chasing after his older brother as he jogged up the trail. Jenny and her husband loaded up the empty kid carrier and trailed behind their sons, feeling like a weight had been lifted—both physically and emotionally.

There are many momentous occasions in the first few years of any child's life, but this was a big day for the Taylor family: Pancake became a hiker. To be sure, his short legs were tired after completing the 3-mile round-trip journey to Goose Creek Falls, but he was more interested in the fun he was having with his brother. He immersed himself in the day's adventure without giving a second thought to resting his weary muscles.

"That day was a turning point," Jenny says. "Cakers moved onto the next phase of his life and we watched it happen."

The bridge! The bridge! We almost made it!
DEREK TAYLOR

THE HIKE

From the Goose Creek Falls Trailhead in the Gordon Titus Parking Area, head for the dirt road situated on the north side of the lot. Almost immediately, the trail begins a brief and gentle climb and the route takes a quick left. Pay attention here since the trail is not well marked at the beginning. After a few minutes, the path will begin its descent to Goose Creek; it's all downhill from here! (Yes, that means the return trip is mostly uphill, but we promise that it isn't too tough.) Continue hiking downhill until you reach a bridge that crosses over Goose Creek. Now you know you are close to the falls! Follow the trail as it veers left and intersects with Goose Creek Trail #353. After this junction, you are just a few minutes away from the dramatic viewpoint of the

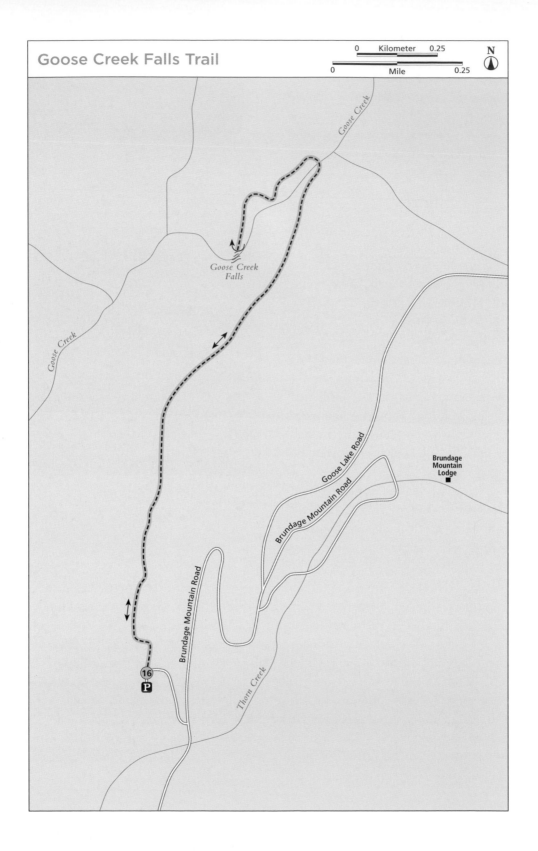

falls. Tip: The final stretch down to the falls themselves is quite steep with loose dirt and rocks, so please be cautious.

MILES AND DIRECTIONS

0.0 Begin hiking on the northside of the parking area.

0.1 Begin descending toward Goose Creek.

1.2 Walk over the bridge as it crosses the creek.

1.3 Trail junction with Goose Creek Trail #353.

1.5 Enjoy the views of the cascading waterfall. Now, it's time to climb! Turn around and retrace your route.

3.0 Arrive back at the trailhead.

SACHI THORNLEY

Lower Calf Creek Falls
Grand Staircase–Escalante
National Monument, Utah

Born and raised on the island of Kauai, Hawaii, Sachi Thornley, 32, grew up with an "outdoor adjacent" lifestyle. Her family didn't specifically enjoy camping or hiking or any of those activities that seem to define the outdoors, but she did spend all of

Sachi Thornley HEIDI SHOMAKER

her time outside. However, her family relocated to Salt Lake City, Utah, when Sachi was in high school. There, her friends introduced her to hiking. She absolutely hated the activity so she continued to avoid it through her high school years. However, her husband, Chad, is an avid outdoorsman. Over time, Sachi realized her lack of interest was preventing her husband from enjoying the activities he loved and she wanted to prioritize his joys. She went out and snagged a permit for the Subway, a famed semi-technical slot canyon hike in Zion National Park. She presented her husband with the permit and said, "So, what's the Subway?!" After that, hiking became a part of the Thornley family fabric.

Sachi is a former team member for Adventure Mamas, a nonprofit dedicated to maternal wellness. While she still holds the organization close to her heart, she had to step away a few years ago when her daughter was diagnosed with cancer. Presently, Sachi has two children: Maddox (13) and Penny (8). She lives with her husband and kids in Salt Lake City.

As one of the more popular and well-known trails in Grand Staircase–Escalante National Monument, Lower Calf Creek Falls is a simple hike that the entire family can enjoy. Lower Calf Creek Falls was relatively unknown to tourists until it (and the surrounding areas) became a national monument created under the Clinton administration. Named for its use as a natural pen for calves back in the late 1800s and early 1900s, this sandy trail takes you along the canyon floor to a 126-foot waterfall outlined in green algae awaiting your tired and hot feet.

Nearest town: Escalante

Getting there: For visitors entering from Escalante on Route 12, drive north about 16 miles to turn left into Calf Creek Campground. You will see day parking as you drive up the short road to the campground.

Trailhead: Lower Calf Creek Falls Trailhead

GPS: N37 47.742' / W111 24.816'

Fees and permits: Parking is $5 per vehicle per day.

Trail users: Hikers, trail runners

Elevation gain: 521 feet

Length: 5.8 miles (out-and-back)

Approximate hiking time: Half day

Difficulty: Easy

Seasonal highlights: Due to the trail's location among the sandstone canyons of the Southwest, hikers have to be careful during monsoon season (July–August) due to flash floods. Always carry plenty of water to ensure enough for the entire hike as it gets dangerously hot and dry.

Managing agency: Bureau of Land Management—Grand Staircase–Escalante National Monument

EXPERIENCING IT

Not all seasons of life involve hiking, and Sachi Thornley is just now reentering her spring.

Even the desert changes colors seasonally HEIDI SHOMAKER

Five years ago, many would argue that Sachi was at the top of her game. A chronically terrible sleeper, Sachi would naturally awake around three in the morning, unable to go back to bed. Instead, she'd quietly tiptoe out of her bedroom, grab her car keys, and point her vehicle toward the mountains lining Salt Lake. She'd spend hours exploring the trails with her girlfriends, ambling through the darkness as the women explored the peaks and valleys of Utah's Wasatch. Rarely did she have a destination in mind. Instead, Sachi simply thrived on the physicality of this new-to-her activity that brought her joy and mental resets. By the time the sun rose and her family began to awaken back home, Sachi was back in the house, replenished and energized after a twilight morning hike. They never even knew she was gone.

Five years ago, the Thornley family was also hitting their stride on the trail. Maddox was 8 years old so he was strong enough to carry a small backpack and navigate his own path. Penny was just 3 but she was independent, even from an early age. Sachi says the family never even purchased a kid carrier; from the day Penny began walking, she wanted to hike her own hike. But this worked for Sachi as she admits the activity never came naturally to her anyway. She encouraged her children to hike through the hardships, reminding them that discomfort on the trail could be normal. "It's okay to feel hungry for a little bit; it's okay to be uncomfortable," Sachi would tell her children as they trekked into the foothills. "Everything is fine."

Sometime after Penny turned 4, it wasn't fine anymore. Sachi remembers Penny crying during one hike, telling her mother that her head and legs hurt. Sachi urged her

The easy trail wraps through quintessential Utah canyon country. HEIDI SHOMAKER

daughter to drink water to help with the altitude headache, but she couldn't make the leg pain disappear. Penny had been born with hip dysplasia and doctors had warned the Thornleys that some discomfort would begin around this age. Sachi chalked the ache up to the dysplasia and encouraged her daughter to walk it off. So she did. But a few weeks later, the family was returning from a trip to California and Penny grew ill. They camped in a lake bed in Joshua Tree National Park, the cracked soil as tattered as Sachi's emotions as Penny violently vomited all evening and into the next morning. It didn't matter what the doctors were telling Sachi anymore; she knew something was wrong.

She was right. Back home in Salt Lake, on a cold February morning in 2017, Penny was diagnosed with a medulloblastoma brain tumor after Sachi rushed her to the hospital. Doctors immediately sedated Penny for surgery, telling Sachi that if her daughter laughed or sneezed one more time, it was likely that a tangerine-size tumor would pop out of the base of her skull. In an instant, Sachi's world flipped upside down. Camping at Joshua Tree didn't matter. Dawn patrol hikes with her girlfriends didn't matter. All that mattered was ensuring she did not lose her daughter.

Thus began the winter of Sachi's life. Penny underwent two brain surgeries to remove the tumor. The first was unsuccessful as the surgeon missed most of it, so the team had to go back in to get the remainder of the malignant mass. Then, the family flew to Washington State, where Penny could receive the proper radiation treatment that was not available in Salt Lake. Unfortunately, Sachi received more bad news upon their arrival in Seattle: In an unprecedented scenario, the Utah doctors had still missed a portion of the tumor. To stand a chance at life, 4-year-old Penny needed a third brain surgery in 2 weeks.

Then, the baby girl underwent thirty rounds of radiation to her brain and spine followed by another nine rounds of high-dose chemotherapy back in Salt Lake.

It was one year of hell. Before Sachi's eyes, her vivacious, independent little girl morphed into a shell of the child she once knew. Penny temporarily lost her ability to walk or communicate, and some days, she didn't even have the energy to sit upright or raise her arm from the hospital bed. Sachi watched her daughter's suffering, unable to do anything other than recycle the same thoughts in her own mind.

If only we hadn't stayed an extra day in Joshua Tree.

If only I had listened when she told me her head hurt.

If only, if only.

Changing leaves in the fall Heidi Shomaker

By the time autumn rolled around, Sachi was depleted. She had yet to leave her daughter's side and her emotional coping skills were nearly gone. Penny was due for another round of chemotherapy when Chad pulled Sachi aside for a conversation.

"You can't be here," he told Sachi. "I know you want to be and I know you will be otherwise, but you are running on fumes and you have been for months. You need to take care of yourself."

In an effort at normalcy, Chad sent Sachi to southern Utah with a few close friends for a camping trip. They loaded the car with plans to road trip from Grand Staircase–Escalante National Monument to Bryce Canyon National Park, camping and day hiking through the beautiful sandstone along the way. And for 2 days, it felt wonderful. Sachi reveled in the

Sachi nearing the waterfall HEIDI SHOMAKER

freedom and lack of invisible responsibility weighing on her shoulders. The fresh air and hot desert sun took her back to an easier time, a time when her family wasn't living on the edge of despair and sorrow and wondering what the next day would bring.

On the third day, Sachi found her way to the Lower Calf Creek Falls trail in Grand Staircase–Escalante. The verdant oasis tucked amidst Navajo sandstone is an iconic southern Utah feature, and Sachi ambled past the prehistoric rock art toward the 214-foot cascade of water. It was a relatively easy hike compared to her past exploits, but it was a warm day. At the base of the falls, she settled into a patch of shade and contemplated her life as she now knew it.

Seated next to the refreshing pool of water sparkling in the late autumn sun, Sachi mentally waged a battle against the dichotomy existing in her mind. She admired her beautiful surroundings and the rejuvenating reprieve that time outside had bequeathed upon her. But simultaneously, her thoughts strayed to Penny, losing her hearing while sitting in a hospital bed undergoing chemotherapy nearly 250 miles away. That's when Sachi made her decision.

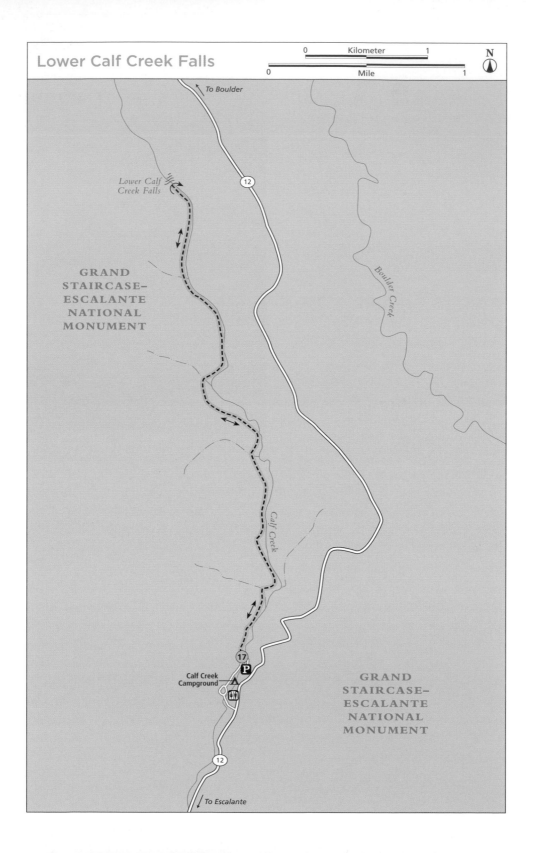

Lower Calf Creek Falls

Lower Calf Creek Falls
Sarah Lamagna

She stood up and stretched her legs before shouldering her backpack and taking a sip of water. Sachi took one last look at the waterfall, searing its beauty into her memory. She didn't know when she would once again be able to visit. Then, she turned on her heels and began the 3-mile hike back to the car waiting at the trailhead. From there, she left her friends and abandoned the trip to return to Salt Lake City and be at her daughter's bedside.

"I remember thinking to myself, 'I really love all of this and it brings me so much joy,'" Sachi remembers. "'But it's okay to pause with this right now; I'll be back.'"

THE HIKE

Begin your hike at the Lower Calf Creek Falls Trailhead at the Calf Creek Campground within Grand Staircase–Escalante National Monument. The trail brings you through Navajo sandstone–covered canyon walls and among several beaver ponds. The hike itself is relatively flat but has stretches of sandy trail that will create some resistance and extra effort on your part. The falls (and subsequent pool) at the end of the hike are a welcome relief for your tired feet.

MILES AND DIRECTIONS

0.0 Begin hiking at the Lower Calf Creek Falls Trailhead just after the Calf Creek Campground.

0.9 Make sure to look up the cliffside and you'll see an old granary (storage structure) built more than 800 years ago.

1.3 Old fence used back in the late 1800s when herding cattle. Just further down are some pictographs seen on the canyon wall.

1.5 Another granary.

2.9 Reach Lower Calf Creek Falls. Retrace your steps.

5.8 Arrive back at the trailhead.

18

KYLEE TOTH

Bow Hut Route
Banff National Park, Alberta, Canada

Kylee Toth, 36, is a professional ski mountaineering racing athlete (skimo) who hails from Vernon, British Columbia, but currently resides in Calgary. Sponsored by La Sportiva and Osprey, Kylee has always been an athlete—although it wasn't skimo that first won her heart. Instead, Kylee competed in high-level speed skating until her early

Kylee Toth KENT TOTH

20s. Then, a friend introduced her to ski mountaineering racing. While it wasn't love at first sight, it did grow on her and she joined the Canadian National Ski Mountaineering Team in 2009. Today, she is arguably one of Canada's top athletes as she works to raise the profile of her sport in her home country. She holds a number of accolades but a few of her crowning achievements include multiple Canadian Female Ski Mountaineering championship titles (2015–2017) and being one-half of the first-ever female team to complete France's Pierra Menta stage race (2017), an annual ski mountaineering competition that includes some of the most important races of the season.

Kylee is married with two sons: Solomon (9) and Zeke (7). When not training, she loves hitting the trails or the ski hill with her family.

The Alpine Club of Canada manages thirty-seven huts across the country and Bow Hut is one of the favorites. The hike boasts incredible views of Bow Lake and the surrounding mountains, but for the best Canadian hiking experience, be sure to book an overnight stay at the hut. This is a self-service structure, which means you won't find five-star dinner service, but the scenery can't be beat. This trail should not be taken lightly, especially during spring runoff (there are several creek crossings) or during the winter (it is well-known for avalanche danger). Regardless of the time of year, the views of the Canadian Rockies at the hut will take your breath away, and you'll soon forget the multiple creek crossings and rock scree scrambles you had to take to get there.

Nearest town: Lake Louise

Getting there: For visitors entering from Banff, drive west on the Trans-Canada Highway 1 until you reach Lake Louise. Exit onto Route 93 North for approximately 36 miles (58 km). Just after Bow Lake, look for signs for the Bow Lake Parking Lot and Simpson's Num-Ti-Jah Lodge.

Trailhead: Bow Hut Route Trailhead

GPS: N51 40.752' / W116 27.864'

Fees and permits: Day-use Banff National Park fees are $10 per person or $20 per family/group. Staying the night at Bow Hut costs $30 per night for Alpine Club of Canada members (and $40 for nonmembers).

Trail users: Hikers, trail runners, backpackers, cross-country skiers

Elevation gain: 2,342 feet

Kylee shouldering the weight while her kiddos run ahead KYLEE TOTH

Length: 9.8 miles (out-and-back)

Approximate hiking time: Full day or overnight

Difficulty: Strenuous

Seasonal highlights: Bow Hut is part of the popular Wapta Traverse cross-country ski route, so this trail can be managed year-round for those who are trained for avalanche safety. As with any high-alpine route, weather moves in quickly during the summer season, so keep an eye on the clouds. Because there are stream crossings, this hike can be quite challenging (if not dangerous) during spring runoff.

Managing agency: Parks Canada–Banff National Park

EXPERIENCING IT

When Kylee Toth competes in skimo, she is a well-oiled machine. Ski mountaineering racing is anything but easy since athletes are required to ascend (on skis or with crampons, depending on the steepness of the mountain slope) nearly 5,000 vertical feet before skiing back downhill again. Not only are the natural elements a factor, but so is the speed. The fastest racers win, so Kylie can't dawdle on her way uphill and she must maintain control at all times in order to prevent disastrous crashes on the downhill. As a result, it's paramount that Kylie heads into each race with deep confidence and a solid strategy for how she wants to carry out her game plan.

But when she hikes with her children, it's an entirely different story.

When her sons were babies, Kylee enacted a tradition: Each year, she would take them on an overnight hike to one of the huts in the Alpine Club of Canada's system. During those early days, she found the shortest hikes possible. But as her sons grew older, Kylee and the boys wanted to tackle grander adventures together. So, in 2019, the three of them set their sights on a new challenge: Bow Hut, a beautifully scenic structure perched above Bow Lake in Banff National Park.

As with all of her athletic accomplishments, Kylee used the 90/10 rule for the adventure: 90 percent of the work happened before she and the kids ever stepped foot on the trail. She spent the preceding week gathering the trio's gear and strategically fitting it all into her own backpack. Since she was strong enough to carry everything, she decided to let her kiddos run wild and play while hiking, unencumbered by heavy loads. After a few hours of driving and wrangling a veritable zoo at the trailhead, Kylee and the boys began their hike.

Or so she thought.

The family had walked *maybe* a third of mile when Zeke plopped down on the ground and proclaimed he didn't want to hike any farther. "I could literally see our car windshield," Kylee laughs. In between her son's grumblings, Kylee learned that

Zeke found his hiking boots intolerable. "Mom, they hurt my feeeeeeet," he exclaimed while prying his finger into the heel of his boot in a valiant attempt to rip the offending item from his tiny foot. With nearly the entire trek in front of them and only the parking lot behind them, Kylee thought fast.

First, she tried reasoning with her child, but to no avail. Zeke held fast with his staunch belief that these hiking boots were the worst things he'd ever worn. In an effort at a peace treaty, Zeke offered a concession and told his mom he would be happy to walk barefoot. When that didn't fly, the duo needed a third plan.

Kylee discovered the solution in Crocs.

Ever the diligent mother, she had packed two pairs of Crocs, the ultralight rubber shoes commonly used as hut booties in the

Glacier-blue waters along the trail KYLEE TOTH

mountaineering community. The nearly plastic shoes weigh so little and bend so easily that it was almost a no brainer for Kylee to slip a few pairs into her massive backpack. Now, she found herself enormously grateful for her own foresight.

"Hey buddy, how do you feel about wearing your Crocs?" she asked her youngest with a slight hint of persuasion in her voice.

Pleasantly surprised that he had won the battle, Zeke readily agreed. Kylee helped her son remove the displeasing and cumbersome boots and replaced them with the slim-and-trim Crocs, ensuring the heel strap was pulled down against her child's foot. She briefly worried at the reality of the situation: How in the world would Zeke hike nearly 10 miles with more than 2,000 feet of climbing in a pair of rubber sandals that had virtually no traction? Ultimately, she decided that was a problem for her future self, and off they went.

TIPS FOR HUT-TRIPPING WITH KIDS

Adventuring to a mountain hut with your children may be one of the best ways to experience the backcountry for the first time. Not only is it a more controlled environment (hello, heat!), but there are also more amenities, like beds and stoves, than found at campsites. These perks can simplify your first trip so you have the bandwidth to worry about other concerns—like how many gummy bears to pack for your child.

Here are four tips to help your family tackle your first hut adventure. Enjoy!

- *Start 'em early.* As with all endeavors, backcountry huts feel more natural to kids if they have grown up with them. Sleeping in a bunkroom doesn't feel abnormal if you've done it a few times!
- *Book a private hut.* Or, if that's not possible, inquire about a private room. Kids' sleeping habits are unpredictable, and it will remove a lot of stress if you know your child's potential middle-of-the-night cries won't waken others in the building.
- *Be choosy with the hut.* Before you go, spend some time researching your hut options. For your first foray, avoid huts where questionable terrain is part of the journey. It's also a good idea to aim low with the mileage rather than challenge your kiddos with their first double-digit hike. It could be the most amazing hut in the world, but if your son only remembers the massive blister on his heel, he won't want to go back for seconds.
- *Pack light.* This goes for parents, too! The biggest mistake most hikers make is bringing too much gear. Not only do you have to shoulder the heavy load, but it's more to manage once you arrive. Be selective and bring versatile pieces that air-dry quickly. After all, no one is judging your apparel when there are mountains of trails to be hiked.

Taking a cue from the first 10 minutes on trail, Kylee built out the rest of the adventure using motivating benchmarks along the way. First, she encouraged the boys to make it to a curve in the lake. Once they arrived, they celebrated with a snack break. Then, she challenged her sons to make it to the waterfall, accompanied by yet another snack break. This continued the entire morning as she sprinkled obstacles and rewards throughout the day in an effort to entertain her children. Their favorite benchmark came just before the 4-mile marker when the family encountered a massive boulder wedged into the gorge. As part of the trail, everyone had to clamor over the top of the 15-foot-wide stone, but the exercise felt truly special to Solomon and Zeke.

"Mom, would you look at this rock?" Solomon bellowed in excitement.

What's a hike without a pair of Crocs? Kylee Toth

Each boy took a turn, holding his mother's hand while practically dancing across the boulder. Once he reached the other side, he looked up expectantly. "Let's go back!"

It wasn't efficient: The trio took over 6 hours to arrive at the hut while Kylee usually does it in 2 when she is solo. But it was fun. And Kylie had learned that these hikes with her kiddos were not the time to be objective-driven. While racing, her modus operandi was all fast, so she did plenty of that in her other life. But these moments

Fooling around in a snow cave KYLEE TOTH

with her boys were special and called for slowing down and spending extra time on embracing the moment. And if it happened in Crocs, so be it.

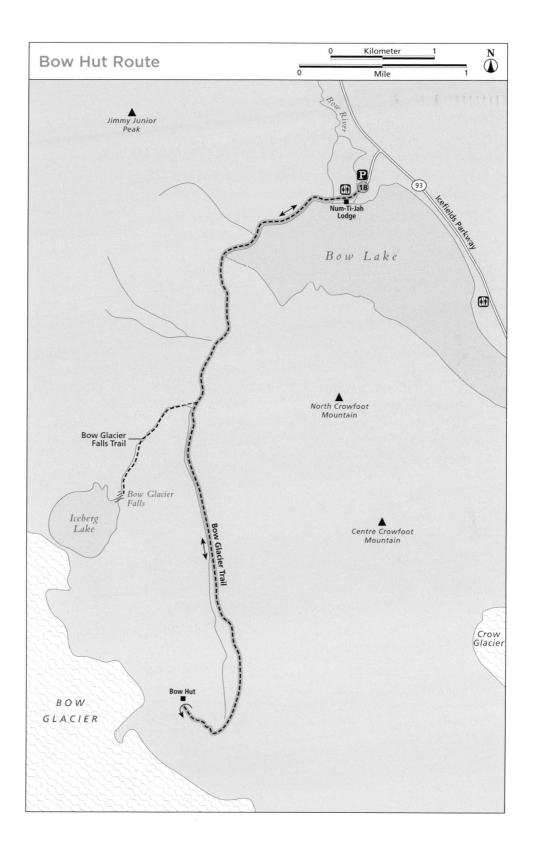

Bow Hut Route

0 Kilometer 1

0 Mile 1

N

Bow River

Jimmy Junior Peak

P 18

93 Icefields Parkway

Num-Ti-Jah Lodge

Bow Lake

Bow Glacier Falls Trail

North Crowfoot Mountain

Bow Glacier Falls

Iceberg Lake

Bow Glacier Trail

Centre Crowfoot Mountain

Bow Hut

Crow Glacier

BOW GLACIER

THE HIKE

Begin your hike at the Bow Lake parking lot just before the Simpson's Num-Ti-Jah Lodge. The first 1.5 miles hug the northern side of Bow Lake before reaching the "end" where a glacial-fed creek comes into view. There are man-made steps straight in front of you heading toward Bow Glacier Falls, but instead, take the trail left over the natural boulder bridge to the other side of the creek. The trail steeply ascends to a moraine basin with a spectacular glacier at the far end of it. This is where you'll first get a glimpse of Bow Hut sitting right on the ridge to the right. Again, you'll have a creek crossing that can be very challenging depending on the season, so pick your route wisely. Remember, if the creek is too swift or too high, it's best to turn around and save the hike for another day. After the creek crossing, it's a moderate scramble up to the hut where you can enjoy whatever beverage you brought in your pack. Head back down the way you came before summer thunderstorms roll in.

MILES AND DIRECTIONS

0.0 Bow Hut Route Trailhead.

2.0 You will see stairs in front of you heading to Bow Glacier Falls, but go left to head to Bow Hut. Scramble up and over boulders to get to the other side of the stream.

3.6 First view of Bow Hut on the ridge to your right.

4.0 There is a challenging stream crossing—there are several routes across, so pick the one that you are most comfortable with.

4.9 Bow Hut. Return the way you came.

9.8 Arrive back at the trailhead.

VERNA VOLKER

Jensen Lake Trail
Eagan, Minnesota

Verna Volker is an ultrarunner from the Navajo Nation; her clans are Tódích'íi'nii (Bitterwater) nishłíí, Hashtł'ishnii (Mud People) bashishchiin, Ta'neeszahnii (Tangle) dashicheii, and Tó' áheedlíinii (Water Flows Together) dashinalí. She is also the mother of four children (ages 7, 11, 14, and 16). While she grew up in in the Dzilnaoodilii area of New Mexico, she now lives in Minneapolis with her kids and her husband of 20 years.

Verna Volker VERNA VOLKER

Professionally, Verna spent many years as a teacher, but became a stay-at-home mom when she had children. Five years ago, she returned to the workforce as a part-time special education paraprofessional in the schools. Verna is also the founder of Native Women Running, a social media organization born out of frustration in 2018. As a decade-long runner herself, Verna quickly noticed the lack of representation of Native women in social media, print media, podcasts, and among sponsored apparel athletes. Knowing many Indigenous runners herself, Verna set out to create a community dedicated to increasing the visibility of Native women while overcoming stereotypes and encouraging each other to stay positive.

Revered as a quiet escape from the bustling city of Minneapolis, Jensen Lake is a good retreat for all ages, all skill levels, and almost all activities. You'll find yourself meandering through aspen trees and hardwood forests while taking in the sight of the wildlife at the lake's edge. If you fancy sitting idle, make sure to bring your fishing rod and enjoy the stillness of the lake regardless of season. If you'd rather have a heart-pumping adventure in the winter, then bring your cross-country skis to enjoy the many trails that are linked up with Jensen Lake. Regardless of your adventure of choice, Jensen Lake provides the landscape to do it all.

Nearest town: Eagan

Getting there: For visitors entering Lebanon Hills Regional Park from the south on I-35E, take exit 93 for Cliff Road. Take a right onto Cliff Road and follow for 1.6 miles. Take another right onto Pilot Knob Road for 0.7 mile. Take a left onto Carriage Hills Drive and then a quick right into the parking lot for Jensen Lake.

Trailhead: Jensen Lake Trailhead

GPS: N44 46.698' / W93 09.942'

Fees and permits: No day-use fees except for cross-country skiers ($6 per day)

Trail users: Hikers, trail runners, cross-country skiers, snowshoers, anglers

Elevation gain: 121 feet

Length: 2.1 miles (loop)

Approximate hiking time: Half day

Difficulty: Easy

Seasonal highlights: Lebanon Hills is pleasant during any season and is a favorite for the local ice-fishing community. The trails are perfect for cross-country skiing.

Managing agency: Dakota County Parks–Lebanon Hills Regional Park

EXPERIENCING IT

Verna Volker wasn't always a runner. In fact, it's a fair statement to say she flat-out disliked the sport since she lived by the expression, "never a runner but always an athlete." She grew up playing outside, running through the sun-drenched sagebrush of New Mexico's Navajo Nation. Her family didn't have a lot of money, but she and her nine siblings found entertainment playing in the dirt or scampering through the canyons and making mud pies with the thick clay soil. She played basketball and volleyball in high school and dreaded the days when conditioning drills and sprint work sat atop the agenda. When she reached college, she dabbled in running as a means to stay active, but it was always something she did out of necessity rather than enjoyment.

But things change and life moves on. After years of bouncing from New Mexico to Missouri, she and her family finally settled in Minneapolis, her husband's home state. Verna stayed busy as she birthed their second child, but she quickly learned she wanted an activity to help regain her fitness. Once again, she reached for running, the trusty standby always hiding in a shadowy corner. She found a local race with distance options: 2.1 miles and 5 miles. Not willing to fully commit to the sport, Verna signed up for the 2.1-mile option and gritted her teeth while enduring the seemingly impossible feat. She even laughs now as she recounts watching the 5-mile runners cruise by on the course. "I remember thinking, 'Why would anyone run that far?!'"

But a few years later in 2009, Verna found herself circling back to the sport that had trailed her throughout life. With all four children born and no plans for more, Verna carried a bonus 50 pounds that she wanted to lose. More important than the weight loss, however, was her mental state. She wanted to be an athlete again. Verna vowed to take better care of herself and capped the promise off with another challenge: a half marathon.

And so it went. One mile led to 2 miles, which led to 13.1 miles and beyond. After running the half marathon, Verna found herself relying on the sport for physical activity and mental release. When she pounded the pavement, she didn't have to worry about her daily routine and life's usual stressors. It was just her, the sidewalk, and her running shoes, nothing more. As her mileage escalated, so did her emotional health. The years ticked by and her distance increased from a half marathon to a full marathon (26.2 miles); then, she tackled a few 50-kilometer (31-mile) ultra-distance races. By 2019, she was ready for her next challenge: a 50 miler.

Verna registered for Surf the Murph, a beautiful 50-mile suburban course largely set on doubletrack trails with a smattering of singletrack sprinkled into the mix. The race is known for its hilly terrain (especially in the Midwest), so Verna knew the uptick in mileage combined with the rugged topography would call for an increase in training. Working with her trainer, Verna hit the trails 5 days per week, logging anywhere from 30 to 50 weekly miles with weekend-long runs of 18 to 20 miles a pop.

Any parent can attest to one thing: There is not a lot of free time in the day. While Verna's four kids were older, she still needed to make a concerted effort to carve out space for her training. During the weekdays, Verna found a routine that allowed her to cram in some miles between her other obligations. She'd awake in the morning, feed her children breakfast, and hustle them off to school. Then, she would zoom home and hop on the treadmill in a time-crunched effort to log some miles before showering and heading *back* to school in the afternoon for her work as a paraeducator. "There was no time anywhere else so I just squeezed miles in wherever I could," she remembers.

Weekends were easier and that's when she typically logged her long runs. And it was during these double-digit journeys that Verna found her groove—and fell in love with the trails.

Each weekend, she connected with her husband to ensure he could handle the kids on Saturday morning. Then, she set her alarm for an ungodly hour, frequently waking

Snapping a quick selfie during her training VERNA VOLKER

at 4 or 4:30 a.m. in an effort to get an early start on the day. After loading up her running pack with fuel and hydration, Verna sleepily laced up her shoes, hopped in the
car, and followed her headlights south to Lebanon Hills Regional Park.

Lebanon Hills Park is the gem of the Dakota County park system, containing five
trailheads within the 2,000-acre park. Verna gravitated toward the Jensen Lake Trailhead where she often began her journey. She'd set foot to trail, easing into a calm pace
as she skirted the banks of Jensen Lake in the quiet darkness of the early morning.
As she listened to the continual *thump-thump* of her own footsteps, she slipped into
a peaceful meditative state. She felt her body warming as her breathing quickened,
awakening her soul better than any alarm clock. By the time she reached the far side of
the glimmering water, her mind had caught up to the rest of her body and encouraged
her to keep moving. So she did.

Verna lived for these Saturday runs. Often, she would run for 8 or 9 hours, navigating her way through the circuitous park system. Sometimes, she ran faster just to see

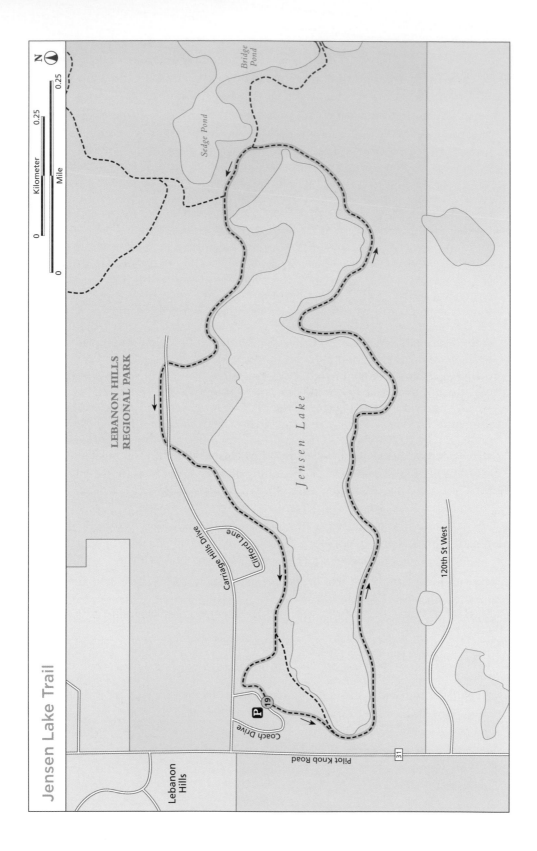

Jensen Lake Trail

how it felt to breathe harder. Other times, she'd slow to a walk, always moving forward while she admired her surroundings and engaged in animated conversation in her mind. Fast or slow, it didn't matter: She just needed time on her feet.

Her 20-milers also provided Verna with time to ponder the universe. The framework of her routine was based on fuel. Per her coach, she needed to ingest water and an energy gel every two hours. In between, she'd pop in her earbuds and enjoy a guilty pleasure: podcasts. She never listened to them while running roads due to safety concerns, so it was delightful to enjoy that luxury on the trails. She'd also think about her children, remembering fun conversations or upcoming events in their lives. During her longest of trail runs, she'd dedicate miles to various family members, including her aging mother or her deceased father or the three sibling she'd lost in past years. In doing so, Verna built in a form of self-resilience. She could finish this mile because she was running for *them*.

But through it all, she kept running. She ran to get away from the stressors of daily life and the incessant reminders of obligations and responsibilities. She ran because these mornings gave her time for herself, a luxury not frequently granted to a mother of four. She gave so much of herself during the work week—whether to her husband or children or students at school—that it felt good to give *herself* this gift: solitude.

And so she ran.

THE HIKE

Begin your hike at the Jensen Lake Trailhead; you can access the trailhead from several parking lots. The trail has minimal elevation gain and traverses along the lake's edge for the bulk of the hike, switching from dirt path to boardwalk whenever the soil and surrounding vegetation is too sensitive for our footprints. On a summer day, you'll see lots of kiddos trying to catch crayfish along the lake's shore while the winter brings out those brave enough to sit still while ice fishing.

MILES AND DIRECTIONS

0.0 Begin hiking along a dirt path at the Jensen Lake Trailhead at the first parking lot.

0.2 Trail hugs the southern end of the lake.

1.0 There is a short side trail that brings you to view the lake from a park bench.

1.2 Reach the easternmost edge of the lake where the trail heads slightly away from the shore.

1.3 Trail brings you back closer to the shore for the last part of the hike.

2.1 Trail ends where you first picked it up.

FELICIA WONG

Vernal Falls via the Mist Trail
Yosemite National Park, California

Felicia Wong FELICIA WONG

Felicia Wong, 41, is a double board-certified emergency and consultation liaison psychiatrist based in Orange County, California. While she now calls the Golden State home, Felicia grew up in a suburb outside of Boston. As a first-generation American, both of Felicia's parents immigrated to the United States from China and spent long hours working to create a stable lifestyle for their family. As a result, Felicia and her brother first experienced the powers of the outdoors by exploring a small nature reserve near their neighborhood. It wasn't anything complicated or elaborate, but Felicia remembers spending her afternoons after school catching tadpoles and playing in the grass. This reserve became her "magical space" where her dreams and imagination knew no bounds.

Today, Felicia is married to her husband, Jason, who is a general surgeon. The couple has two children—Alex (7) and Brian (5)—who have been hiking with their parents since they were babies.

Easily one of the most accessible trails in all of Yosemite National Park, the Mist Trail to Vernal Falls is still a heart-pumping excursion full of quad-busting elevation gain and jaw-dropping views. In the heart of Yosemite National Park's valley, the trail rises up on one of nature's grand staircases with Vernal Falls cascading beside you. Hot summer days are the best time to view the falls since you're bound to get splattered with the waterfall's mist. You can link up this trail with several more including another waterfall (Nevada Fall) or the John Muir Trail to make this an all-day adventure.

Nearest town: Mariposa

Getting there: For visitors entering Yosemite National Park from the west on Route 140, continue onto El Portal Road after the entrance station. Follow this road for 5.5 miles and then take a slight right onto Southside Drive. Continue for 6.1 miles, where the road turns into Happy Isle Loop Road. You will see the trailhead parking on your right. If taking the shuttle, it'll be Shuttle Stop #16 (Happy Isles Trailhead).

Trailhead: Happy Isles Trailhead

GPS: N37 44.100' / W119 33.972'

Fees and permits: Day users need an America the Beautiful Interagency Pass ($80 per year) or a Yosemite National Park day pass ($35 per vehicle).

Trail users: Hikers, trail runners

Elevation gain: 1,279 feet

Length: 3.0 miles (out-and-back)

Approximate hiking time: Half day

Difficulty: Moderate

Seasonal highlights: Since the hike brings you to the top of a beautiful waterfall, the best time to visit this trail is during spring runoff (April–June) when the falls are profusely pouring over the edge.

Managing agency: National Park Service–Yosemite National Park

EXPERIENCING IT

Although Felicia Wong did not grow up in a stereotypically outdoor family, she readily credits her childhood for today's love of nature. When her parents arrived in the United States for graduate school, they came with a suitcase full of clothing and nothing else. Thanks to borrowed money and old-fashioned sweat equity, they built a life for their family in Boston. It wasn't glamorous but it was honorable hard work, a trait they both seemed to carry in unlimited quantities. They each worked the equivalent of two full-time jobs, spending 7 days per week toiling away at their professions. But still, they were attentive parents, ensuring Felicia and her brother were enrolled in a myriad of after-school programs designed to better themselves both personally

Three generations exploring Yosemite National Park FELICIA WONG

and professionally. In addition to her homework, Felicia remembers a laundry list of extracurricular activities: Sewing, cooking, art, musical instruments, ballet, and varsity swimming were all hobbies that filled her schedule during her youth. Moreover, her parents expected her to remain in touch with her cultural heritage, so Felicia also enjoyed traditional Chinese dance and played the Chinese dulcimer (as well as the piano and the viola).

Free time was virtually nonexistent, but when the family could slip away for the predetermined 2 weeks of vacation every year, they would road-trip to various national parks. Hiking was always on the agenda, albeit differently than how it is for Felicia and her children now. When the family vehicle pulled up to Acadia or Yellowstone National Park, Felicia, her parents, and her brother simply got out and began walking. They didn't own hiking shoes, nor did they wear any high-tech apparel or carry fancy backpacks. They didn't have any special outdoor gear whatsoever. Instead, hiking was about enjoying the scenery—and anyone could do that regardless of special gear.

But all of that began to change for Felicia when she was a senior in high school. She was selected to represent Massachusetts at the National Youth Science Camp in West Virginia. For 3 weeks, she and the other nominees enjoyed scientific immersion, during which their days were filled with lectures on everything from astrology to the dissection of the human hand to growing strawberries in Chile. For fun, the camp also offered various outdoor excursions via hiking, caving, whitewater kayaking, and backpacking. Felicia signed up for two hikes: a 15-miler and her first overnight backpacking trip. As a gift, her parents purchased her first pair of true hiking shoes, complete with noticeable traction and sturdy lateral support. Felicia was hooked.

Smiling for the camera! FELICIA WONG

A QUICK HISTORY OF YOSEMITE NATIONAL PARK

With nearly 4.5 million visitors annually, Yosemite ties with Zion National Park for the fourth most-visited national park in the United States. Clearly, people love visiting Yosemite, but most may not know the long history behind their favorite protected wilderness area. Today, the beating heart of the park is Yosemite Valley, and science tells us that people have lived there for more than 3,000 years. The Ahwahnechee are a Miwok people first associated with the valley, which they called Ahwahnee, or "gaping mouth-like place." By the late 18th century, the majority of Yosemite was inhabited by Southern Miwok people, but that changed in the late 1700s as non-native people began arriving to the area. By the mid-1800s, the California Gold Rush brought thousands of miners to the Sierra Nevada, all desperate and ruthless in their search for gold. In 1851, a state-sponsored militia known as the Mariposa Battalion entered Yosemite, making multiple attempts to remove the Miwok people from the area, but they were unsuccessful. Still, more people came. By 1864, a group of conservationists convinced President Lincoln to declare Yosemite Valley a public trust, marking the first time the government protected land for public enjoyment. In 1889, John Muir began lobbying for national park status, which was granted in 1890 (and the park was subsequently transferred from state-controlled to government-controlled status in 1906). However, life began to change for the Indigenous people in the valley as a result of all of these protections. Clothing and food styles changed and new employment opportunities arose. By the early 1900s, the number of Native people living in the valley began to diminish. As housing became more problematic, more Natives left. The last Native homes in the new Indian Village were razed in 1969. Today, descendants of Yosemite's Native people live in surrounding areas, as well as throughout the world.

Her life was still on autopilot in another direction, but she carried that experience with her to Brown University where she was accepted to medical school straight out of high school. But in her first year, she herniated a disc in her spine that devolved into excruciating lower back pain. For the next 2 years, she suffered to the point where getting out of bed caused tears and taking herself to the restroom felt like an exercise in stress management. Outdoor adventure was placed on hold as she even had to take a temporary break from her studies. But still, Felicia is able to look back on that time and see the silver lining.

"It made me resilient," she remembers. "Those years helped me find some toughness."

The beautiful Vernal Falls
FELICIA WONG

Time passed and Felicia finished her schooling and subsequent residency. As she neared the age of 30, she looked at her husband and told him: "It's always been my dream to live in California, so let's do it."

There, the Wong family grew with the addition of their two sons. And as Felicia established her career drawing from the hardworking, multitasking ethics her parents had taught her as a child, she also began incorporating her love for adventure into the family routine. It was one of these trips that found Felicia, her husband, her children, and her parents at Yosemite National Park's Vernal Falls on a three-generation adventure.

Ever the mama bear, Felicia approached the hike just like she does with her career. She evaluated all of the potential fail points, including the steep terrain and the fall of darkness. Always a scientist, Felicia also routinely evaluates what she refers to as the "rate limiting factor." Taken from chemistry, the original meaning references the slowest step in a chemical reaction that determines the overall time. For example, one can quickly pour a gallon of water through a funnel, but the rate limiting factor is actually the width of the funnel since it determines how fast the water flows. On her family hikes, Felicia always identifies the rate limiting factor so she can set an appropriate schedule for the day. For Vernal Falls and its steep topography, she determined that the family would have to move at the pace of her youngest son. Although they had hiked a number of other trails in the park, her parents opted to sit this one out.

With more than 1,200 feet of gain in just 1.5 miles, Vernal Falls is a literal walk in the park that is anything but leisurely. But still, Felicia's children headed up the trail full of enthusiasm and excitement for the journey ahead. Every corner turned brought a series of "That's so cool!" choruses from Alex and Brian. Felicia felt a deep satisfaction seeing her sons actually enjoying the process. The boys bounded from rock to rock, scrambling over larger boulders and sprinting ahead when they wanted to race. At one point, Felicia and Jason found themselves hurrying just to keep pace with their youngest son. By the time the family had reached the misting waterfall, everyone was sweaty and smiling with gratification. In fact, her youngest wanted to continue: "Mom, can we keep going to Nevada Falls?" he begged with imploring eyes.

But his grandma and grandpa were waiting back in the valley, so the Wong family turned and headed back to the trailhead rather than continuing. As she hiked downhill, Felicia reflected upon the generational conglomeration that had assembled itself along the path. Her parents hiked to attain a goal: a rewarding vista or a towering mountaintop summit. Clearly, their influence was present within her boys, so eager to reach their "destination" at the top of the waterfall. But while Felicia thrived on achieving those mile markers, she also took great pleasure in enjoying the journey and respecting the process, yet another characteristic she admired in her sons as they marveled at the trailside geography. This concept of dualism—the yin and the yang, if

The Wong family posing in front of Vernal Falls FELICIA WONG

you will—appears to be a philosophical contradiction. But as Felicia watched her boys veritably dance down the trail toward their waiting grandparents, she understood that it wasn't about contrarianism. Everything was interconnected, and her kids are living proof of that.

THE HIKE

Begin hiking along the road (only open to pedestrians, cyclists, and cars with disability placards) to the start of the Happy Isles Trailhead. As this is one of the more popular trails in Yosemite National Park, get here early for parking or take the park shuttle until stop #16. Although this trail is short, it gains a lot of elevation in a short amount of time, so make sure you are physically prepared for the trek up to the waterfall. The first mile is paved and brings you to the Vernal Falls Foot Bridge. Here, you can either stop and snap some photos of the falls or head the rest of the way up the falls to get a stunning view of the Yosemite Valley. We recommend the latter!

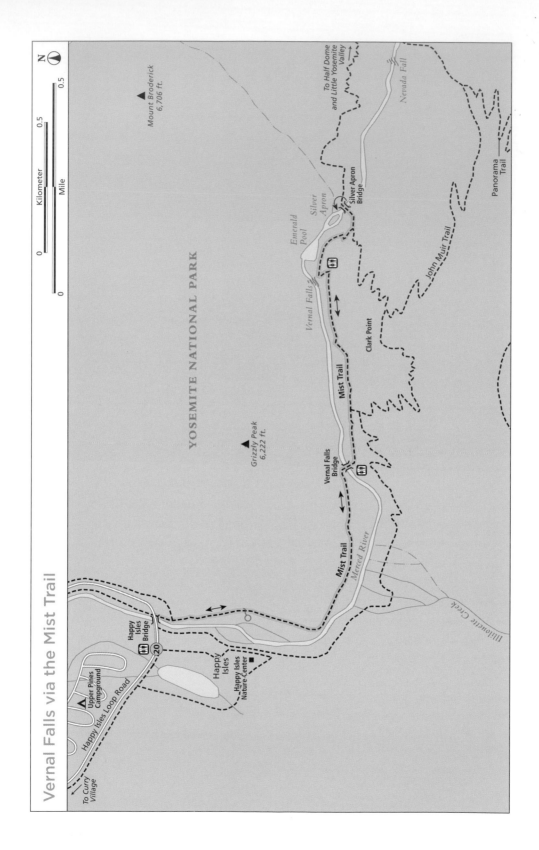

Vernal Falls via the Mist Trail

N

Kilometer
0   0.5   0.5

Mile
0   0.5

To Curry Village

Upper Pines Campground

Happy Isles Loop Road

Happy Isles Bridge

20

Happy Isles

Happy Isles Nature Center

YOSEMITE NATIONAL PARK

Grizzly Peak
6,222 ft.

Mount Broderick
6,706 ft.

Mist Trail

Merced River

Illilouette Creek

Vernal Falls Bridge

Mist Trail

Clark Point

Vernal Falls

Emerald Pool

Silver Apron

Silver Apron Bridge

John Muir Trail

To Half Dome and Little Yosemite Valley

Nevada Fall

Panorama Trail

MILES AND DIRECTIONS

0.0 Begin hiking along the road/bike path to link up with the Happy Isles Trailhead.

1.0 Reach the Vernal Falls Foot Bridge.

1.2 Reach the John Muir Trail junction. Keep on the Mist Trail.

1.4 Trail becomes very narrow and potentially very wet from the waterfall's spray.

1.5 Reach the top of Vernal Falls. You can continue a short way to Emerald Pool (do NOT jump in the water as the current is extremely strong and dangerous). Retrace your steps and head back to the trailhead.

3.0 Arrive back at the trailhead.

Index

About the Author

Heather Balogh Rochfort is a freelance writer and author of three books: *Backpacking 101*, *Sleeping Bags to S'mores*, and *Women Who Hike*. She is a frequent gear writer for REI and has bylines in publications like the *Washington Post*, *Afar*, *Men's Journal*, *Backpacker*, *Outside*, *Sierra*, and more. Heather is also the cofounder of WildKind, a digital membership community dedicated to engaging and educating families to get outside in a meaningful way. An enthusiastic hiker, backcountry skier, backpacker, and trail runner, she lives in Carbondale, Colorado, with her husband, daughter, and rescue dog.